SEBZE

To my dear parents,
Orhan and Gülçin,
and to our beloved
Antakya

Vegetarian recipes from my Turkish kitchen

SEBZE

Özlem Warren

PHOTOGRAPHY BY SAM A HARRIS

Hardie Grant

BOOKS

Ekmek, Börek, Pide
BREAD AND SAVOURY BAKES ——————— 29

Kahvaltı
ALL-DAY BREAKFAST ——————— 53

Çorba
SOUPS ——————— 71

Meze ——————— 87

Salata
SALADS ——————— 113

Zeytinyağlı
VEGETABLES COOKED IN OLIVE OIL ——————— 133

Sokak Yemekleri
STREET FOOD ——————— 159

Pilav, Bulgurlu, Mercimekli Tatlar
WHOLEGRAINS, PULSES AND RICE ——————— 177

Ocak ve Fırın Yemekleri
CASSEROLES, STEWS AND PASTA ——————— 191

Turşu, Salça ve Soslar
PICKLES, CONDIMENTS AND SAUCES ——————— 211

Kek, Kurabiye, Tatlılar
SWEETS ——————— 223

Merhaba and *Hoş Geldiniz*

My warm welcome to you all

Since the declaration of the republic on 29 October 1923, my homeland has always been known to us Turks as *Türkiye* (officially, *Türkiye Cumhuriyeti*), commonly known as Turkey (or the Republic of Turkey), worldwide. In 2021, via the United Nations, the government officially replaced Turkey with *Türkiye*. In *Sebze,* I will lead with the name *Türkiye* followed by the English translation.

It is an absolute privilege to share with you the delicious, wholesome vegetarian cuisine of my homeland. 'Sebze' means 'vegetable' in Turkish, its roots derived from the Persian *sabze* or *sabzi*, meaning 'greenness'.

Seasonal produce has been a focal part of Turkish cuisine, along with legumes and wholegrains, for centuries. Paying tribute to our glorious, varied fresh produce, *Sebze* is a bountiful collection of scrumptious, practical and diverse vegetarian recipes. My cooking has always been inspired by this magical land and the warm spirit of Turkish culture. *Sebze* is my invitation for readers to embrace the vibrancy, simplicity and generous nature of our vegetarian cuisine and our rich culinary heritage.

I have long wanted to write this book. Living abroad for six years in the USA and 15 years in the UK, I've seen how Turkish cuisine is mostly associated with kebabs, and that many are unaware of the different ways we enjoy seasonal vegetables, legumes and wholegrains. In *Sebze*, I am passionate about sharing our vast array of vegetarian and vegan dishes, which were a huge part of my diet growing up. One of my fondest memories were the daily trips to the farmers' market (*pazar*) in Istanbul with my dear father, Orhan, to pick up the fresh vegetables and fruits on offer, chatting with vendors and making sure to stop by the *gözleme* (stuffed flatbreads) stall for a nice snack with a glass of *çay* (Turkish tea). Coming home excitedly with juicy tomatoes, vibrant aubergines (eggplant) or whatever produce was on offer, my dear mother, Gülçin, would turn them into tasty casseroles (*türlü*) or aromatic pilafs, incorporating vegetables with bulgur, rice, freekeh or pulses. We would enjoy these with an array of dips, salads and pickles. My family was not vegetarian, but the majority of our diet has always been based on vegetables, mostly cooked in olive oil as in our *zeytinyağlı* (see Chapter 6, page 132) and incorporated into soups, casseroles and *meze*. These were not only delicious, but wholesome and good value, too. I hope you will find much inspiration in *Sebze* for how we prepare and enjoy vegetables, legumes and grains flavourfully and with ease.

The healthy Mediterranean diet is an important influence in Turkish cooking, with its plentiful use of fruit and vegetables, pickled and dried vegetables (to enjoy out of season), olive oil, wholegrains and nuts. Seasonality and flexibility are crucial to the way we cook, and Turkish cuisine is naturally rich in wholesome, practical and good-value choices for a vegetarian and plant-based diet. Like my family, many are now keen to incorporate more vegetables and grains into their diet for their wellbeing, as well as for the planet. I believe the recipes in *Sebze* will not only please vegetarians, but also anyone who would like fresh and achievable vegetable-centred ideas to include in their cooking.

Zero waste and making use of leftovers have been important features of Turkish cuisine for centuries. The recipes in *Sebze* not only complement one another but make use of leftovers to create more flavourful, good-value meals. Do have a go at *Otlu Tava Böreği* (Easy, Herby Pan Börek, page 40), for instance, to use up leftover filo pastry and any fresh greens you have to hand.

The majority of Turkish recipes can be prepared ahead of time and freeze well – we all live busy lives and this helps so much to plan and prepare appetising and nourishing meals. You will find most recipes in *Sebze* include advance preparation tips, freezing options and variations for gluten-free and plant-based diets, when applicable (see Dietary Keys on page 26).

It has been my passion to teach Turkish cookery for 20 years around the world and I always encourage students to take the recipes as guidelines and make them their own. With rising food costs, we are all mindful of our expenditures; Turkish cuisine and the recipes in *Sebze* are flexible and remind you to make use of ingredients you have to hand and to substitute when necessary.

My Southern Turkish Roots

Antakya in southern *Türkiye* (Turkey) has been home to my family for over five generations. Our beloved hometown, along with a large part of the southeast of the country, was severely damaged during the February 2023 earthquake. It broke our hearts to lose loved ones and witness the severe damage to a very special place we call home. As Antakya and the surrounding area are now starting to recover, I wanted to introduce this special land and my roots briefly. It shaped who I am and my cooking immensely.

My mother Gülçin and father Orhan were both from Antakya. Ahmet, my grandfather on my father's side, was a soap maker (the family name Sabuncu means 'soap maker'), creating Antakya's highly-regarded olive oil soaps. Suphi, my mother's father, was a respected food merchant, trading fresh and dried produce within the city and across the border with Syria. Generosity and abundance were an important part of daily life; I fondly remember the excitement of Suphi dede (Grandpa) delivering cases of figs, aubergines (eggplant) and tomatoes to the family home, which we shared with friends and neighbours.

I was lucky enough to spend many happy childhood holidays at my grandparents' 450-year-old stone house in Antakya. This was a warm, special home: pomegranate, fig, mulberry and walnut trees filled the courtyard, with wafting smells of Grandma (Nazime) making molasses from pomegranates, or Mum making *dolma* with Grandpa's peppers and aubergines, under the welcoming shade of the trees. Nazime nene (Grandma) would send us grandchildren to Uzun Carşı, the city's historic market, to buy cheese, daily bread and yoghurt – I loved walking on the cobbled streets, taking in all the mesmerising smells, colours, and daily banter from the merchants.

I was born and raised in *Türkiye* (Turkey) and feel fortunate to have lived in this magical land with its rich heritage and warm culture for 30 years. I grew up with wholesome, freshly prepared meals using seasonal produce, and the importance of sharing was instilled in us from an early age. My dear father, Orhan, had endless generosity; he loved going to our local farmers' market (*pazar*) regularly, bringing home fresh produce. Once I moved abroad, he would mail monthly care packages of nuts (we have the most flavourful nuts [*çerez*]) from Istanbul to the UK, which were eagerly awaited by my husband Angus. There were also Turkish delights and treats for the children.

For my dear mum, Gülçin, cooking and feeding loved ones was her way of showing her love. Despite being a busy science teacher, she would cook lovely meals for us from scratch, repurposing leftovers and using storecupboard ingredients. At the weekends, she would batch-cook casseroles (*türlü*) and vegetables in olive oil (*zeytinyağlıs*), showing us how convenient Turkish cuisine can be, with its ahead-of-time preparation. Watching her make mouth-watering meals with such economy and ease has been a huge inspiration for me, and is a key foundation block for *Sebze*.

My nickname: *Patlıcan*

Turkish food is such a big part of our lives that giving loved ones food-related names as a term of endearment is not unusual in Turkish culture. My father would call my mother *canım*, *ciğerim* (meaning 'my dearest, my liver').

I left home in 1995 to pursue my master's degree in Scotland where I met my husband Angus. Angus, without being aware of this tradition, decided to call me *patlıcan* (meaning aubergine/eggplant) during the very early days of our courtship. *Karnıyarık* (stuffed aubergines), was the first dish I cooked for him and its preparation involved a lengthy and expensive phone call from Scotland to my mother in Istanbul. As I was getting *karnıyarık* tips from my mother, Angus overheard and asked what *patlıcan* meant. After I had translated, he said: 'it sounds rather nice, I think I will call you *patlıcan*!' It became my nickname between us from then on, or sometimes just *patlı*, and I hold this with affection.

After six years of a long-distance relationship (and to my parents' delight), we got married in Istanbul. I first moved to the UK with Angus, and then we moved to the US. Living abroad, I greatly missed Turkish food and the generosity and warmth of our culture. Cooking was a way for me to reconnect with loved ones and my homeland, and so it was a joy when I discovered the Central Market Cooking School in Austin, Texas, where I could channel my passion. With the cookery school's encouragement, I started to teach Turkish cookery in Austin, Houston, Dallas and San Antonio. I am forever grateful to Central Market and their support for Turkish cuisine and their belief in me. I absolutely love teaching not only my homeland's vibrant cuisine but also talking about the culinary traditions of my bountiful land. Upon moving back to the UK in 2009, I continued to travel and teach in the US, UK, *Türkiye* (Turkey) and Jordan regularly, as well as hosting supper clubs and culinary tours to my homeland.

My Southern Turkish Roots

My Turkish roots define the person that I am today, and it is a great honour to be able to share the bounteous delights of Turkish vegetarian cuisine through *Sebze*. In many ways, this book is taking my cooking full circle, back to that childhood, where I was surrounded by an abundance of fresh, seasonal produce, and where repurposing and sharing that food was our way of life.

Turkish Cuisine

Turks were nomadic tribes that lived in Central Asia from the 6th century AD. Their food was mainly based on meat, grains and dairy. The extensive use of yoghurt, *yufka* (thin filo sheets) and *mantı* (dumplings) dates back to this period. By the 11th century, Turkish nomads had settled in Anatolia, the mainland of today's *Türkiye* (Turkey).

Anatolia was home to ancient civilizations prior to the arrival of nomadic Turks – Hittites, Urartians, Persians, Ancient Greeks and Eastern Romans all flourished on this land. Upon settling in Anatolia, nomadic Turks formed the Seljuks and through interaction with Arab-Iranian, Byzantine and other settled communities in Anatolia, new culinary habits started to emerge. But it was the formation of the Ottoman Empire in the 14th century which provided the major contribution to Turkish cuisine. The Ottomans conquered vast amounts of land and built magnificent palaces, such as the Topkapı Palace in Istanbul. Lavish banquets and ceremonial meals on special occasions were of great importance to the Ottomans, as they were an opportunity to showcase the power of the state. Charity was also important, with the palace kitchens distributing food to the poor during religious festivals. By the 16th century, the grand kitchens of the Topkapı Palace employed 1,300 staff who would serve thousands of people every day. There were chefs who specialised in different categories of dishes, such as the *börekçi*, savoury pastry chef; *baklavacı*, the maker of sweet pastries; and *tursucu*, the pickle-maker.

At its peak, the Ottoman Empire stretched from Eastern Europe, to southern Russia, from North Africa to the Middle East, with many ethnic communities living together for centuries. Each community brought their own authentic ingredients and flavours to the palace kitchens and helped create a shared culinary heritage, which further enriched Turkish cuisine. The Sultan also controlled the spice route, as he commanded his merchants to trade only the highest-quality spices. By the 18th century, new, fresh ingredients had been introduced to the palace kitchens over time, such as tomatoes, peppers, potatoes, and courgettes (zucchini) – all of which are widely used and much loved in Turkish cuisine today.

The modern Republic of *Türkiye* (Turkey) was founded by Mustafa Kemal Atatürk in 1923. Today, Turkish cuisine encapsulates a mosaic of rich, diverse culinary heritage, balancing the past, present and a rich tapestry of regional cuisines.

Regional Turkish flavours

Türkiye (Turkey) is surrounded by the Aegean, Black Sea and the Mediterranean, has diverse climates and fertile soil, and various ethnic communities that have all helped shape regional cuisines. Seasonal, fresh produce is consumed throughout the country and in many regions excess produce is pickled, turned into paste or dried to be used out of season.

The Marmara and Istanbul region carries the legacy of the Ottoman palace kitchens and its ethnic communities. *Meze*, vegetables cooked in olive oil, pickles and a variety of milk- and pastry-based desserts are all a legacy from the Ottoman period. You can also find fine examples of regional flavours in Istanbul, as the city is made up of migrants from across the region. Christian, Jewish, Muslim, Greek, Armenian and Kurdish residents of the city

all contribute to the local cuisine. The city has a vibrant street food scene, along with bakeries and *esnaf lokantası* (casual, buffet-style restaurants) serving sweet and savoury delicacies with regional and ethnic flavours.

Mainland Anatolia has a harsh climate and the cuisine is largely based on wheat, legumes, dairy, savoury pastries and mutton. Eastern and southern Anatolian cuisine is rich in bulgur-based dishes, as well as kebabs, flavourful condiments, such as pomegranate molasses and pepper paste, and local cheeses. Gaziantep in southeastern Anatolia grows some of the finest pistachios and is home to the best baklava. The climate is hot and dry in summer, perfect for drying and preserving. Şanlıurfa in the region is famous for its smoky isot (*Urfa* chilli pepper). The Black Sea region produces the nation's tea leaves, hazelnuts, corn and collard greens, along with the much-loved anchovies (*hamsi*). The milder climate in the Aegean and the Mediterranean lends itself to seasonal fruit and vegetables, olives, herbs and wild greens. There is a variety of seafood and wines from this region.

Home of wheat

Türkiye's (Turkey's) culinary heritage also shows hidden traces of the Neolithic period, dating back to 10,000 BC. Anatolia is regarded as the home of wheat – very early human settlement has been discovered at the UNESCO World Heritage site Göbeklitepe in the southeast. This ancient site reveals important clues that show wheat was first cultivated here and played an important role in the transition from nomadic to settled life. Today, the Anatolian soils provide a home for over 20 species of wild wheat, which is reflected in the variety of our breads.

Sustainability and zero waste

Turkish culture has practised sustainability and zero waste for centuries. When peppers and tomatoes are in abundance, they are turned into paste and pickles. When there is an excess of aubergines (eggplant), courgettes (zucchini) and okra, they are dried over the terraces of village homes to be used in the winter in the south.

Bread is sacred and stale bread is always repurposed into another dish. Turkish bakeries (*fırın*) in Anatolia act as 'the community oven' and will bake your stuffed flatbreads, casseroles and *dolmas* in a wood-fired oven, saving you energy at home. I have fond memories of trips to our local *fırın* to pick up our stuffed flatbreads, *Ispanaklı Katıklı Ekmek* (page 46). Preparing stuffed vegetables is another good example of no-waste Turkish cuisine.

For example, while preparing *Bulgurlu Lahana Sarması* (stuffed cabbage rolls, page 146), we also make a dish called *Kapuska* (a cabbage stew) with the leftover chopped hard stalk and smaller leaves of the cabbage and cook them in the same pan. So, you get two dishes in one, saving time and energy and using up almost all of the cabbage.

What to expect in *Sebze*

There are 85 scrumptious vegetarian Turkish recipes in *Sebze*. We have a rich and diverse regional cuisine, which I have researched extensively. *Sebze* includes lesser-known regional specialties along with popular Turkish recipes and a few of my own creations. Many of the recipes complement one another and leftovers can be repurposed for other delicious meals with ease. Let's have a short glimpse at the *Sebze* chapters:

Ekmek, Börek, Pide

Bread and savoury bakes are an essential part of Turkish cuisine and there is a generous selection in this first chapter, from *Kabaklı Kol Böreği* (page 32) to *Balon Ekmek* (page 44).

Kahvaltı

All-Day Breakfast is one of my favourite chapters; you can enjoy herby *Kaygana* crêpes (page 58) to *Çılbır* (page 61) at any time of the day.

Çorba

The Soups chapter offers wholesome and great-value options using store-cupboard ingredients, including regional specialties such as *Pazılı Lebeniye Çorbası* (page 74).

Meze

The *Meze* chapter covers delightful, do-able recipes that complement one another for a *meze* feast. Please have a go at *Nar Ekşili, Cevizli Pancar* (page 92); it is a taste sensation and leftovers can be repurposed in *Pancarlı Nar Ekşili, Firik* (page 185).

Salata

The Salads chapter showcases the bounty of our farmers' markets (*pazar*). Our salads are substantial with inclusion of nuts and legumes, for example *Tahinli Fasulye Piyazı* (page 120).

Zeytinyağlı

The *Zeytinyağlı* chapter highlights our time-honoured, simple and nourishing approach to cooking vegetables in olive oil, where recipes can be prepared ahead of time. From my husband's favourite *Zeytinyağlı Biber Dolması* (page 144) to *Zeytinyağlı Pazı* (page 156), there is something for everyone here.

Sokak Yemekleri

The Street Food chapter includes mouthwatering examples from our Turkish street vendors. You will be pleasantly surprised how easy and satisfying it is to make the iconic *Simit* (page 168) in your kitchen.

Pilav, Bulgurlu, Mercimekli Tatlar

The chapter on Wholegrains, Pulses and Rice covers a variety of ways we enjoy these staples at home; try the Ottoman palace specialty *Kestaneli İç Pilav* (page 189); this regal pilaf is so easy to make.

Ocak ve Fırın Yemekleri

The Casseroles, Stews and Pasta chapter is home to our comfort food, with dishes that you can make with ease, such as *Fırında Patates Paçası* (page 208), scrumptious garlicky mashed potatoes, Turkish-style. *Nohutlu Tepsi Mantısı* (page 204) will impress your guests, and is a practical feast too, as you can prepare it ahead.

Tursu, Salça ve Soslar

We Turks are pickle (*turşu*) lovers, so you will find a variety of pickle recipes, including *Patlıcan Turşusu* (page 214), along with condiments and sauces to enhance your dishes.

Kek, Kurabiye, Tatlılar

Finally, Sweets take centre stage in Turkish cuisine. From the Turkish classic milk-based *Fırın Sütlaç* (page 235) to the easy and fragrant *Kuru Kayısı Tatlısı* (page 231), there is something for everyone. And let's not forget pumpkin and walnut baklava, *Balkabaklı, Cevizli Havuç Dilimi Baklava* (page 226) – a lighter and impressive baklava, my own creation, which I hope will be a showstopper at your dinner parties.

Sebze is a recipe collection built with convenience and flavour in mind, inspired by my homeland's rich and diverse culinary heritage. I hope you will embark on a culinary journey to my homeland, to discover a selection of delightful, achievable vegetarian recipes.

From my kitchen to yours – *Afiyet Olsun*, as we say in Turkish – may you be happy and healthy with this food.

Essential Ingredients

The majority of ingredients in *Sebze* are widely available these days through supermarkets or online. A few specialty ingredients can be bought through Turkish, Mediterranean or Middle Eastern stores, or online (see page 247). Here are some of the key ingredients from my kitchen.

Olive oil

Probably one of the most used ingredients in my kitchen, olive oil is life for us. *Türkiye* (Turkey) produces some of the finest olive oil in the world and I use it every day. We even have a whole category of vegetables cooked in olive oil called *zeytinyağlı*. Extra-virgin olive oil is mostly used for salads, dips and *meze*.

Olives

We are a nation of olive (*zeytin*) lovers. A short trip to a farmers' market (*pazar*) would give you a dozen varieties of olives, all bursting with flavour. I prefer to buy mine unpitted, as these tend to have better texture and taste.

Beyaz peynir

Our much-loved brine cheese, made from unpasteurised sheeps', cows' or goats' milk, is an essential part of the Turkish breakfast. The Turkish brand Pınar is my favourite. You can substitute with a good-quality, creamy feta.

Yoghurt

Yoghurt forms an important part of the Turkish diet, dating back to the nomadic Turks. Gut-friendly yoghurt is served with almost every meal and there is a tub in the refrigerator of every Turkish home. Use in soups, marinades, dips and desserts, or enjoy at breakfast with fruit, nuts or honey.

Nuts

Some of the world's finest nuts are grown in my homeland (pistachios in Gaziantep, hazelnuts in the Black Sea region and almonds throughout the country) and they are a major staple in my kitchen. We eat these wholesome snacks daily and use them in our salads, desserts and meals.

Dried fruit

Many fruits, especially apricots and figs, are dried to be used out of season. We eat them as healthy snacks and enjoy them in salads, desserts, jams and pilafs.

Yufka (filo pastry sheets):

These thin unleavened sheets of dough have ancient roots going back to the nomadic Turks, who used to make thin *yufka* bread over an inverted pan called *sac*. Today, fresh *yufka* sheets are widely available and are an everyday essential at home. Outside *Türkiye* (Turkey), filo sheets provide a good substitute for *yufka*, especially for savoury pastries and *börek*. For making baklava, thinner filo sheets (*baklavalık yufka*) work best, although I have often made decent baklava with regular filo sheets, too.

Chickpeas (garbanzo beans), dried beans and lentils

Legumes are an essential part of my pantry. Dried beans and chickpeas are more widely available these days, offer great value and I use them often. Having said that, I always keep tins of good-quality pre-cooked beans and chickpeas in my kitchen as they are convenient and wholesome. When it comes to lentils, I prefer them dried rather than pre-cooked, as they have better texture and nutrition and are widely available.

What to Expect in Sebze

Bulgur

I love the nutty taste of bulgur; it's wholesome and so easy to cook – a must in my kitchen. Bulgur wheat is a grain made from cooked wheat berries that have the outer bran case removed and are then dried and pounded. It's widely available in supermarkets these days. Fine bulgur (*ince bulgur*) is finer ground and lighter in texture, which is great in salads and patties. You can find fine bulgur in Turkish and Middle Eastern shops as well as online.

Freekeh

Smoky freekeh (*firik*) is an ancient super grain made from unripened green durum wheat. Nutty freekeh pairs beautifully with bulgur and vegetables and is widely available in supermarkets, Turkish and Middle Eastern shops and online.

Maize flour/cornmeal

Corn flour (*mısır unu*) is a vital staple in the Black Sea region. Made from milled, dried corn, traditional *mısır unu* has a slightly gritty texture. Maize flour (also known as corn flour, *not* cornflour/cornstarch) or fine cornmeal is a good option and is available in supermarkets and health stores.

Turkish red pepper paste

Biber salçası is a pepper paste made from juicy and spicy red peppers, and is an essential condiment in southern Turkish cuisine. It is a versatile ingredient and a little bit of it adds oodles of flavour to casseroles, salads and dips. Sweet and hot pepper paste are two commercially available varieties (the hot pepper paste can be quite spicy, so do bear that in mind) and the Turkish brand Öncü is my favourite. It is available in Turkish and Middle Eastern stores and online. You can also make your own pepper paste with my recipe on page 218.

Pomegranate molasses

Pomegranate molasses (*nar ekşisi*) is another much-loved condiment in the south, made from fresh pomegranate juice, which is reduced to a thick, rich molasses. Its naturally sweet and tangy flavour is fantastic in salads, dips and marinades. It is also widely available in supermarkets and online these days, although it's worth paying a little extra for the best quality. Odysea and Punica Sadece Nar are my favourite brands. I also included my recipe for homemade pomegranate molasses on page 220 if you would like to make it at home.

Tahini

Tahini (*tahin*) is a rich, earthy paste made from toasted, crushed sesame seeds; we widely use it in dips, salads, breads and cookies. Please stir tahini before using as it tends to separate into oil and solids in the jar.

Turkish coffee

Türk kahvesi is one of my favourite hot drinks. It is more than a drink for us with its traditions and rituals, and we use it in coffee cakes, too (see my recipe on page 236). It is made from 100 per cent Arabica beans toasted to the roasting point and ground to a very fine powder. Turkish and Middle Eastern stores and specialty stores online carry Turkish coffee.

Cumin

Ground cumin (*kimyon*) is widely used in Turkish cuisine and in my kitchen. I adore its pungent, warm aroma. It pairs beautifully with vegetables and legumes, and is wonderful in marinades.

Dill

Fresh dill (*dereotu*) is a versatile, aromatic herb; it adorns our vegetables cooked in olive oil (*zeytinyağlıs*) and flavours *meze* and dips.

Mint and dried mint

Mint (*nane*) is a versatile, refreshing herb, commonly used in salads, refreshing drinks like lemonade, and dips. Dried mint is especially popular in southern Turkish cuisine and is used liberally in soups, bulgur-based dishes and casseroles.

Parsley

Maydanoz is the most widely used herb in Turkish cuisine. We use the flat-leaf variety at home (called Italian parsley in the US). Parsley adds a neutral, clean and almost citrussy taste and we use it liberally in salads, *meze*, soups and stews.

Pul biber

Also known as Aleppo pepper, *pul biber* is probably the most used spice in Turkish cuisine. You'll always find a small pot of *pul biber* next to the salt and black pepper for everyday seasoning on our tables. It has a mild, pleasant heat and a warm, smoky taste and adds depth of flavour to dishes. On the other hand, *Urfa biber*, also known as *isot pepper*, from the Urfa region, is salty, spicy, has a purplish black colour and a deeper, smokier flavour than *pul biber*.

Sumac

I love the citrussy, tangy flavour of sumac, or *sumak* as we call it. It is coarsely ground and has a vibrant, purple colour. You can season your salad with sumac as you would with lemon or vinegar. It is fabulous on grills (broils), too.

Za'atar

Zahter is a popular herb and spice blend mostly used in southern Turkish cooking. The herb *zahter* looks more like a summer savoury, or a crossing of marjoram, oregano and thyme. In southern *Türkiye* (Turkey), dried *zahter* blend is a rich mixture of the crushed *zahter* herb with sesame seeds, crushed cooked chickpeas (garbanzo beans), cumin, nigella seeds, sea salt, sumac and more. In my hometown, Antakya, locals enjoy dipping their bread into olive oil and then into the *zahter* for breakfast – it's a real treat. It is also fantastic in salads and marinades.

A Few Tips

My biggest joy as a cookery teacher has always been seeing recipes inspire folks to have a go. Many express how pleasantly surprised they are, discovering just how easy it is to cook delicious and healthy Turkish food. Here are my few tips as a cookery teacher that I try to highlight throughout the book, too.

Go hands on

One of the things we practise every day is combining ingredients with our hands, feeling the produce, trusting and assessing it with our senses. I watched my mother and grandmother combining vegetables with olive oil and spices by hand; rubbing sumac into the onions when making *piyaz* salad, noticing how the onion softens and how the sumac is infused. This method not only ensures that the ingredients blend well for maximum flavour, but it also provides a sensory, satisfying cooking experience.

Be flexible in the kitchen

I always treat my recipes as guidelines, hoping to inspire and excite readers. We may not always have all the ingredients that a recipe calls for (and we may not enjoy some), therefore I encourage you to be flexible in the kitchen, substituting with other ingredients that are to hand. Throughout *Sebze*, I offer ideas for substitutes in the hope that you enjoy making the recipes your own way and use up ingredients.

Experiment with spices

We are lucky to have access to a huge variety of spices nowadays. Turkish cuisine uses spices to flavour dishes naturally, but without overpowering them. Please experiment with spices, perhaps using a little more than you ordinarily would do to flavour your dishes. Pungent cumin, warming *pul biber*, zingy sumac and refreshing dried mint are all staples in my kitchen and can elevate your dish with minimum effort.

Love your leftovers

The Turkish kitchen is a zero-waste kitchen by tradition, and leftovers are repurposed to make other equally tasty meals with ease and economy of time and budget. Many recipes in *Sebze* give suggestions to make the most of leftovers in a delicious, wholesome way.

Embrace preparing ahead

Most Turkish food can be prepared ahead of time and freezes well. This helps to provide nourishing meals with ease and according to your own schedule.

Last but not least, please have a go

Get out of your comfort zone and try a new recipe or a new ingredient, even though it may appear a little daunting at first. I have provided simple instructions in *Sebze* that I hope will help.

Dietary Keys

(GF) Gluten-free

(V) Vegan

(VO) Vegan option

(GO) Gluten-free option

Ekmek, Börek, Pide

One

Bread and Savoury Bakes

Ekmek, Börek, Pide

B reads (*ekmek*), savoury pastries and *börek* (pies made with *yufka*/filo sheets) are an indispensable part of Turkish cuisine. Every neighbourhood has *pastanes* (patisseries), *börek* and *pide* shops that sell these savoury treats, along with *fırın* (local bakeries). These were a dear part of my childhood: the mesmerising smell of my mother's *börek* used to greet us as we returned from school in the afternoon, and if my Grandma was making *Ispanaklı Katıklı Ekmek* (page 46) that would mean an adventure to the *fırın* in Antakya. We would wait with huge excitement while the flatbreads were cooking in the baker's oven, and the bonus treat was sampling a small piece on the way back home.

Savoury bakes are very popular at home and one of my favourite things to eat. I have a generous collection in this chapter, including Coiled Filo Pie with Courgette, Dill and Feta (page 32) and Easy, Herby Pan Börek (page 40), ideal to finish up leftover filo sheets and ingredients to hand. As for breads, or *ekmek*, they are the main pillars of Turkish cuisine, traditionally accompanying every meal. Please do have a go at my easy puffy breads, *Balon Ekmek* (page 44); they are ready in no time and a must at a *meze* table. I am also excited to share some Black Sea specialties: *Mısır Ekmeği* (Corn Bread, page 50), vital and much loved in the region; and Trabzon *Yağlı Pide* (page 48), a feast in itself with oozy melted cheese over soft *pide* with an egg cracked on top.

Turkish savoury pastries are incredibly versatile and can be enjoyed as part of a brunch, starter, snack or light supper – I find they make a day just that little more special. They can be prepared ahead, are freezer friendly, and I offer ideas for substitutions where possible. I hope they tempt you to have a go – you will be pleasantly surprised to see how easy and delicious they are.

Kabaklı Kol Böreği

Coiled Filo Pie with Courgette, Dill and Feta

Serves 4~6

This moreish coiled filo pie is always a hit with family and friends, and looks impressive to serve. We have many varieties of this coiled *börek* and this filling has Mediterranean and Aegean flavours. There is a lovely natural sweetness from the courgettes (zucchini), which complements the saltiness from Turkish *beyaz peynir* (feta cheese) so well.

7 filo pastry sheets
(270 g/10 oz; 48 x
25cm/19 x 10 in),
thawed if frozen
1 tablespoon sesame
seeds

FOR THE FILLING
2 medium–large
courgettes (zucchini)
(485 g/1 lb 1 oz), trimmed
and grated
2 tablespoons olive oil
1 medium onion, finely
chopped
200 g (7 oz) Turkish *beyaz*
peynir **or feta,** drained
and crumbled
1 small bunch of dill,
finely chopped
1 teaspoon *pul biber*
sea salt and freshly ground
black pepper, to taste

FOR BRUSHING
2 tablespoons milk
1 medium egg, beaten
1 tablespoon olive oil

FOR GLAZING
1 medium egg, beaten
2 teaspoons olive oil

FOR THE FILLING, place the grated courgette in a colander and sprinkle with salt. Set aside for 10 minutes. Using a clean dish towel or sturdy paper towels, squeeze out the excess juice (this is an important step, otherwise this excess juice would make the pastry soggy). Place the prepared courgette in a large bowl.

Heat the olive oil in a wide heavy pan over a medium heat, add the onion and sauté for 8 minutes until softened. Stir in the courgette, sauté for another 4 minutes, then season with salt and pepper, and transfer to a mixing bowl. Stir in the crumbled cheese, dill and pul biber. Check the seasoning – you may not need additional salt, as the cheese is already salty. Leave to cool for about 10 minutes.

Preheat the oven to 180°C fan/200°C /400°F/gas 6. Line a round baking dish, 25 cm (10 in) in diameter, with baking paper.

Combine the ingredients for brushing in a small bowl. In a separate bowl, mix the beaten egg and olive oil for glazing.

Open your filo pastry sheets, gently lay them on a dry, clean surface and cover with a damp towel to keep them moist. Take only two sheets at a time and keep the rest covered under the damp towel. Lay two filo sheets on top of each other on a clean, dry surface. Brush the top sheet with the milk, egg and olive oil mixture.

Place about 145 g (5 oz) of the filling in a line, along the long edge near you, leaving 2 cm (¾ in) at each end filling free (take care not to overfill so that the pastry stays intact). Gently roll up into a cylinder. Brush the pastry edge with the milk, egg and olive oil mixture. Starting from one end, gently wind the filo into a coil and place in the centre of the baking dish. Brush the top and sides of the coiled pastry with the egg, milk and olive oil mixture (this also helps to patch up any broken pastry).

Repeat the same procedure with the next four filo pastry sheets, using two sheets at a time. Coil each filo cylinder around the previous one to make a larger spiral. Make sure to brush the top and sides of the coiled pastry with the egg, milk and olive oil mixture. Fold the last remaining filo sheet in half and brush with the egg, milk and olive oil mixture. Place the remaining filling in a line along the edge and roll up again into a cylinder. Coil around the previous one to complete the spiral. Brush the top and sides of the coiled pastry with the egg, milk and olive oil mixture and patch up any broken pastry.

TO FINISH, brush the top and visible edges of the pie with the glaze mixture and sprinkle the sesame seeds over. Bake for about 35 minutes until the top is golden brown and cooked through. Let it cool for 5 minutes, then slice into wedges to serve.

+ **Prepare ahead:** This can be prepared two days ahead. Keep covered in the refrigerator or freeze, gently wrapped in foil. You can reheat in a 180°C fan/200°C/400°F/gas 6 oven for 8–10 minutes (from chilled) or 15–20 minutes (from frozen) until piping hot.

+ **Variations and serving suggestions:** Instead of courgettes, you can also use spinach, sautéed leeks, kale or Swiss chard. And please use up any cheese you have to hand. Serve with *Kısır* (page 130).

Patlıcanlı Rulo Börek

Filo Rolls with Aubergine, Pepper and Onion

Makes 18

This is a popular *börek* especially enjoyed in the summer months at home, showcasing our beloved aubergine (eggplant), *patlıcan*. Fresh, thin *yufka* sheets are traditionally used at home, though the filo pastry works well in this recipe with the meaty aubergine filling and makes a delicious, satisfying treat, great for entertaining.

7 filo or *yufka* pastry sheets (270 g/10 oz; 48 x 25 cm/19 x 10 in), thawed if frozen
1 tablespoon sesame seeds
1 teaspoon nigella seeds

FOR THE FILLING
2 large or 3 medium aubergines (eggplant), cut into 1 cm (½ in) cubes
5 tablespoons olive oil
1 medium onion, finely chopped
1 red and 1 green bell pepper, deseeded and finely chopped
2 tablespoons double concentrated tomato paste
sea salt and freshly ground black pepper

FOR BRUSHING
1 medium egg, separated
25 ml (1 fl oz/scant 2 tablespoons) full-fat milk
2 tablespoons olive oil
25 ml (1 fl oz/scant 2 tablespoons) sparkling water

Spread the cubed aubergines on a large tray, sprinkle with salt and leave for 10 minutes (the salt will help draw out excess moisture). Using a paper towel, gently squeeze the excess moisture out of the aubergines.

Heat 3 tablespoons of the olive oil in a large wide pan, add the aubergines and sauté over a medium–high heat for 10–12 minutes until the aubergines are softened and starting to char around the edges. Transfer to a large mixing bowl to cool.

Heat the remaining 2 tablespoons of olive oil in the same pan and sauté the onion and peppers for 10 minutes, stirring often – they will soften and start to brown a little around the edges. Add to the bowl with the aubergines, then stir in the tomato paste, season with salt and pepper and gently combine. Leave to cool for 10–15 minutes.

FOR THE BRUSHING MIXTURES, combine the egg white with the milk, 1 tablespoon of the olive oil and the sparkling water. In a separate bowl, beat the egg yolk and mix with the remaining tablespoon of olive oil.

Preheat the oven to 180°C fan/200°C/400°F/gas 6. Line a baking sheet with baking paper.

Once the filling is cool, open your filo sheets. Place on a dry, clean surface and cover with a damp towel so they won't dry out. Take one filo sheet and, working fast, brush with the milk glaze. Top with another sheet of filo and brush again. Place about 200 g (7 oz) of the filling in a line, along one of the long edges. Gently roll up into a log, not too tight, sealing the ends of the pastry with the milk glaze. Place on the prepared baking sheet and brush the top and sides with the milk glaze. Repeat with the remaining filo sheets and filling, spacing the logs 2 cm (¾ in) apart. For the last filo sheet, cut in half lengthways and use the remaining 100 g (3½ oz) filling. Slice each log into 8 cm (3 in) rolls (or smaller if you prefer). (Ensure you do this before baking, as it will be difficult to cut the crispy filo rolls afterwards.) Brush the rolls with the egg yolk mixture and sprinkle with sesame and nigella seeds.

Bake for 20 minutes, or until golden and crunchy. Cool the rolls for 5 minutes and serve warm or at room temperature.

+ **Prepare ahead:** You can prepare the filling a day ahead, keeping it covered in the refrigerator.

+ **Freezer friendly:** Once baked, you can wrap the rolls in one layer of cling film (plastic wrap) and keep in the freezer. Reheat in a 180℃ fan/200℃/400℉/gas 6 oven for 6–7 minutes.

+ **Serving suggestions:** *Patlıcanlı rulo börek* makes great party food with the *Haydari* dip (page 98). We also love it as part of a Turkish breakfast, brunch or with a cup of tea (*çay*). For a more substantial meal, you can pair with *Nohut Piyazı* (page 118).

Ispanaklı Gül Böreği

Coiled Rose Pastries with Cheese and Spinach

Makes 6

Ispanaklı gül böreği was one of my favourite savoury treats as a child. My mother would serve these with *çay* (Turkish tea) at her ladies' afternoon parties, or as part of *meze* for dinner gatherings. The sweetness from the caramalised onions complements the sharp, tangy *beyaz peynir* (feta) and works well with the spinach in the filling. This *gül böreği* is a real crowd pleaser.

12 filo pastry sheets
(2 x 270 g/10 oz packs;
48 x 25 cm/19 x 10 in),
thawed if frozen
2 teaspoons golden
sesame seeds
1 teaspoon black sesame
seeds

FOR THE FILLING
2 tablespoons olive oil
2 medium onions, finely
chopped
300 g (10½ oz) spinach,
roughly chopped
285 g (10 oz) Turkish *beyaz*
***peynir* or feta,** drained and
crumbled
freshly ground black
pepper, to taste

FOR BRUSHING
60 ml (2 fl oz/¼ cup)
whole milk
4 teaspoons olive oil
1 medium egg, beaten

Heat the olive oil in a heavy wide pan, add the onions and sauté for 10 minutes over a medium–high heat, stirring often, until softened and starting to caramelise. Transfer to a large mixing bowl to cool and stir in the spinach and crumbled *beyaz peynir* or feta. Season with pepper to taste (I don't tend to add salt as the feta is quite salty). With clean hands, combine all the filling ingredients – this will soften the spinach and help the filling to blend well.

FOR THE BRUSHING MIXTURES, combine the milk and 2 teaspoons of the olive oil in a small bowl. In a separate small bowl, mix the beaten egg with the remaining 2 teaspoons of olive oil.

Preheat the oven to 180°C fan/200°C/400°F/gas 6. Line a large baking sheet with non-stick baking paper.

Open your filo pastry sheets, gently lay them on a dry, clean surface and cover with a damp towel. Take only two sheets at a time and keep the rest covered under the damp towel. Lay two filo sheets on top of each other on a clean, dry surface. Brush the top sheet with the milk mixture. Place about 110 g (3¾ oz) of the filling in a line, along the long edge near you, leaving 2 cm (¾ in) at each end filling free (take care not to overfill so that the pastry stays intact). Gently roll up into a cylinder. Brush the pastry edge with the milk mixture. Starting from one end, gently wind the filo into a coil and place on the baking sheet. Brush the top and sides of the pastry with the milk mixture.

Repeat the same procedure with the remaining filo pastry sheets and place the coiled pies on the baking sheet with about 2.5 cm (1 in) between them. Make sure to brush the top and sides of the coiled pastries with the milk mixture to keep them intact.

Brush the top and sides of the pastries with the egg mixture all over and then sprinkle with the golden and black sesame seeds. Bake on the middle shelf of the oven for 25–30 minutes until the tops are golden brown and cooked through.

Serve warm or at room temperature.

+ **Prepare ahead:** You can prepare the filling ahead of time and keep covered in the refrigerator. The pastries can also be baked ahead of time and freeze well. If freezing, reheat in a 180°C fan/200°C/400°F/gas 6 oven for about 8 minutes.

+ **Serving suggestions:** You can serve these delicious rose pastries with the *Haydari* dip (page 98) and/or with the refreshing *Nar Ekşili Zeytin Salatası* (page 66). If you have any filo sheets left, you can wrap with cling film (plastic wrap) and keep in the refrigerator or freezer – they would be brilliant to use for my *Otlu Tava Böreği* (page 40).

Otlu Tava Böreği

Easy, Herby Pan Börek

Serves 4

The idea for this delicious *börek* is to use up ingredients to hand – leftover bits of cheese (grated mild Cheddar works well) or any fresh greens, such as spinach or herbs; my mum would make it using her leftover *yufka* (our fresh filo sheets). In the Aegean region, local greens such as nettle and sorrel are used, too. Cooking the *börek* in a pan is easy and saves time and energy.

4 tablespoons olive oil, for greasing
7 filo pastry sheets (270 g/10 oz; 48 x 25 cm/19 x 10 in), thawed if frozen

FOR THE FILLING
200 g (7 oz) *beyaz peynir* **or feta,** drained and crumbled **(or grated cheese of your choice)**
4 spring onions (scallions), trimmed and finely chopped
1 tablespoon finely chopped dill
2 teaspoons finely chopped fresh mint leaves
2 tablespoons finely chopped parsley (leaves and stems)
2 tablespoons olive oil
sea salt and freshly ground black pepper, to taste

FOR BRUSHING
1 medium egg, beaten
1 tablespoon olive oil
70 ml (2½ fl oz/5 tablespoons) full-fat milk
55 ml (2 fl oz/¼ cup) water

Place all the filling ingredients in a large bowl. With clean hands, season and give it a good mix.

In a small bowl, beat together the ingredients for brushing with a fork.

Brush the base and sides of a 24 cm (9½ in) non-stick pan with 2 tablespoons of olive oil.

Place the filo sheets on a clean, dry surface and cover with a couple of damp paper towels. Cut the sheets to fit into your pan with about 1.5 cm (⅔ in) overhang. Place a sheet in the pan and brush with a tablespoon of the egg glaze. Layer in another sheet and brush as before. Tear three of the filo sheets into pieces and layer about half of them on top of the pastry base, brushing liberally with the glaze (about 4 tablespoons), making sure it covers all the cracks in the sheets as this will keep pastry moist and intact. Spread the filling evenly over the pastry base, leaving 1 cm (½ in) around the edges clear.

Top with the remaining torn pastry sheets and brush liberally with the glaze. Finally, place the two remaining large pastry sheets over the top and brush with the remaining glaze, tucking the edges in to seal the *börek*.

Cook over a low–medium heat for 8–10 minutes until the bottom is golden and crispy. Brush a large flat plate with 1 tablespoon of olive oil. Place the plate over the pan and carefully flip the *börek* over onto the plate. Brush the pan with the remaining 1 tablespoon of olive oil. Gently slide the uncooked side of the *börek* onto the pan and cook for another 7–8 minutes, or until golden and crispy. Transfer to a plate to cool for 5 minutes, then cut into wedges to serve.

+ **Serving suggestion:** Refreshing *Bostana Salatası* (page 127) is lovely with this easy *börek*.

Patatesli Sodalı Börek

Börek Traybake with Onions, Potato and Sparkling Water

Makes 12 slices

This delicious and substantial *börek* is a hit with my family. *Beyaz peynir*, our creamy feta, is traditionally used and it is a lovely match to the caramelised onions and cumin-spiced mash. You can use up leftover mashed potatoes, as well as any cheese you have; finely chopped spring onions (scallions), spinach, or olives would be delicious alternatives, too. The sparkling water in the glaze here brings a springy touch; it puffs up the *börek* slightly and gives a delicious crispness.

1 tablespoon olive oil, for greasing

2 x 270 g (10 oz) packs of filo sheets (48 x 25 cm/ 19 x 10 in)

1 medium egg, beaten

1 tablespoon golden sesame seeds

1 tablespoon black sesame seeds

FOR THE FILLING

700 g (1 lb 9 oz) small–medium potatoes

1 teaspoon ground cumin

3 tablespoons olive oil

2 medium onions, finely chopped

½ teaspoon *pul biber*

1 small bunch of parsley (about 25 g/1 oz), finely chopped

200 g (7 oz) *beyaz peynir* or feta, drained and crumbled

sea salt and freshly ground black pepper, to taste

FOR BRUSHING

1 medium egg, beaten

110 ml (4 fl oz/½ cup) whole milk

2 tablespoons olive oil

90 ml (3 fl oz/⅓ cup) sparkling water

Slice the small potatoes in half and larger ones into three pieces. Place in a medium pan of hot, salted water, partially cover and cook over a medium heat for about 20 minutes until cooked through. Drain in a colander and cool, then peel away and discard the skins. Place in a large mixing bowl, season with salt and ground cumin, and mash with a potato masher or a large fork.

Meanwhile, heat the olive oil in a wide pan, add the onions and sauté over medium–high heat for 12–14 minutes, stirring often, until caramelised. Season with salt, pepper and *pul biber*, then leave to cool.

Combine the cooled onions with the mashed potato in the mixing bowl, and stir in the chopped parsley and crumbled feta. With clean hands, give everything a good mix.

Combine the beaten egg, milk, olive oil and sparkling water for brushing in a small bowl.

Preheat the oven to 180°C fan/200°C/400°F/gas 6.

Grease the base and sides of a 20 × 30 x 5 cm (8 × 12 × 2 in) baking dish with olive oil. Open the filo sheets, place on a clean, dry surface and cover with a damp towel. Cut the filo sheets to 20 x 30 cm (8 × 12 in) to fit into the baking dish; combining two of the smaller-size offcuts to make one big sheet; working this way, you will have 21 sheets. Place two big sheets in the greased dish and brush with 2 tablespoons of the milk mixture. Then layer in the smaller sheets (combining two each to make one large sheet) and brush with the milky mixture every two layers until you reach the 11th sheet. Brush again with the milky mixture and evenly spread over the filling. Keep on layering and brushing with the milky mixture every two sheets. Place the last sheet, pour in the remaining milky mixture and brush, tucking the edges in.

Slice the *börek* into 12 slices and let the milky mixture penetrate all through the slices. Brush with the beaten egg and sprinkle with the golden and black sesame seeds. Let the *börek* soak up the liquid for about 10 minutes, then bake for 30–35 minutes until golden on top. Leave to cool for 10 minutes, then serve warm.

+ **Prepare ahead:** You can bake the *börek* a day ahead and keep covered in the refrigerator. You can also freeze the cooked slices in a single layer in a tightly sealed freezer bag. Reheat in a 180°C fan/200°C/400°F/gas 6 oven for 8–10 minutes.

+ **Serving suggestion:** Serve with *Karışık Mevsim Salatası* (page 124) for a refreshing accompaniment.

Balon Ekmek
Easy Puffy Bread

Makes 6

We Turks have a love affair with these easy puffy breads. They are a must at our *meze* table, traditionally served with butter and crumbly cheese. I love the ease and lightness of this bread; it only has a few ingredients and is ready in almost no time.

175 g (6 oz/scant 1½ cups) **self-raising flour**, plus extra for dusting

145 g (5 oz/generous ½ cup) **natural full-fat Turkish or Greek yoghurt (or plant-based alternative)**

pinch of salt

1 teaspoon **olive oil**

melted butter or olive oil, for brushing (optional)

Combine the flour, yoghurt, salt and ½ teaspoon of the olive oil in a large bowl. Using your hands, mix until combined into a dough. Transfer the dough to a lightly floured, clean surface and knead for 3 minutes until you achieve a soft, smooth dough. Knead in the remaining ½ teaspoon olive oil and form into a ball. Place in a bowl, cover and rest for 10 minutes.

Divide the rested dough into 6 equal pieces and roll into small balls. Lightly flour the work surface and use a rolling pin to roll each dough ball out to a thin disc, 16 cm (6 in) in diameter. Place the discs on a lightly floured surface, next to one another.

Heat a wide, non-stick pan until it is really hot. Keeping it over a high heat, place one of the breads onto the hot pan. As soon as bubbles start to appear, turn the flatbread over. Turn every 30—40 seconds a few times and it will start to puff up. Once light golden bubbles appear and the bread is well puffed up, transfer to a large plate. You can brush with olive oil or melted butter if you like. Cook the remaining breads in the same way and stack on top of each other. Cover with a dish towel to keep moist.

+ **Tips:** Make sure you use a wide, non-stick pan to cook these flatbreads and the pan needs to be hot before you place the dough in it.

+ **Serving suggestions:** Try these easy puffy breads with various *mezes*. They also go very well with *Nohut Dürümü* (page 164).

+ **Variation:** You can use creamy plant-based Greek-style coconut yoghurt for the vegan option. It puffs up slightly less, but makes an equally delicious, soft flatbread.

Ispanaklı Katıklı Ekmek

Stuffed Flatbreads with Olive Oil, Feta and Spinach

Serves 8–10

These fragrant and oh-so delicious stuffed flatbreads are a specialty from my hometown, Antakya. I have fond memories of watching my grandmother preparing the filling in her garden under the pomegranate tree, which we would take to the local bakery (*fırın*) to be baked over the baker's dough – a ritual I loved growing up.

I used my dear mother Gülçin's dough for this homemade version. It is a lovely, soft dough, *kulak memesi kıvamında* as mother would say, meaning 'as soft as your earlobe'. Crumbly *çökelek*, a sort of drier form of cottage cheese, is traditionally used in the filling, although crumbled *beyaz peynir* or feta works well too, combined with spinach, onion and spices.

FOR THE DOUGH

480 g (1 lb 1 oz/scant 4 cups) plain (all-purpose) flour, plus extra for dusting

7 g (¼ oz/1 sachet) instant dry yeast

1 teaspoon sea salt

120 ml (4 fl oz/½ cup) warm full-fat milk

180 ml (6 fl oz/¾ cup) warm water

90 ml (3 fl oz/scant ½ cup) olive oil, plus extra for shaping

FOR THE FILLING

1 medium onion, finely chopped

200 g (7 oz) spinach, coarsely chopped

2 tablespoons olive oil

1 tablespoon double concentrated tomato paste

1 tablespoon Turkish red pepper paste (*biber salçası,* see page 218 for homemade)

1 teaspoon ground cumin

1 teaspoon *pul biber*

200 g (7 oz) *çökelek, beyaz peynir* or feta, drained and crumbled

sea salt and freshly ground black pepper, to taste

Combine the flour, yeast and salt in a large bowl. Stir in the warm milk, warm water and olive oil and knead to combine. Lightly flour a clean, dry surface and turn the dough mixture out onto it. Knead for 2–3 minutes until you have a soft, smooth dough. Grease the bowl with about a teaspoon of olive oil and place the dough in it, cover with cling film (plastic wrap) and a dish towel and leave in a warm place to rise for 1 hour until doubled in size.

Combine all the filling ingredients except for the cheese in a large bowl. Using your hands, knead the mixture to combine everything well – this also softens the onions and wilts the spinach. Add the crumbled cheese and combine well. Check the seasoning, adding more salt or spices to your taste, then set aside.

Preheat the oven to 200°C fan/220°C/425°F/gas 7. Line two baking sheets with baking paper. Pour 3 tablespoons of olive oil into a small bowl and have it near you, along with the filling.

Place the risen dough onto a lightly floured surface, cut in half and knead into two dough balls. Lightly flour the surface again, dip your fingers into the olive oil and gently press out one of the dough balls to a disc, 25 cm (10 in) in diameter. Spoon half of the filling mixture in the middle of the disc of dough and gently spread, leaving 4 cm (½ in) clear around the edges. Dip your fingers in the oil and gently fold the edges of the dough in to enclose the filling. Seal and place the stuffed dough on a floured surface while you repeat this procedure with the remaining dough ball and filling.

Place one of the stuffed doughs in the middle of a baking sheet. Dip your fingers into the oil and gently stretch the stuffed dough into a wide flatbread, 27 cm (11 in) in diameter. A little bit of filling may come out, but don't worry – this is a part of the character of *Ispanaklı Katıklı Ekmek* (although gently close if larger parts of filling are exposed). Repeat with the other dough on the second baking sheet. Bake for 17–18 minutes until golden and cooked through.

Once baked, take the trays out of the oven. Brush the breads with the remaining olive oil and cover with a clean dish towel for 10 minutes to keep soft. Slice into wedges and serve.

+ **Prepare ahead:** You can prepare the filling a day ahead and keep covered in the refrigerator.

+ **Serving suggestion:** These flatbreads are amazing served with soup; enjoy them with the refreshing *Terbiyeli Sebze Çorbası* (page 79).

+ **Freezer friendly:** These baked flatbreads freeze well, too. Slice in wedges and wrap in one layer of foil. You can reheat in a 180°C fan/200°C/400°F/gas 6 oven for 7–8 minutes.

Trabzon Yağlı Pide

Trabzon-Style Pide with Cheese and an Egg Yolk

Makes 2

This is such a delicious *pide* – oozy, buttery, melted cheese over soft *pide* with an egg cracked over – a dish you can eat all day long. The Black Sea region is famous for their variety of *pides* – almost every city has their own specialty *pide* and this Trabzon *yağlı pide* stands out for me. It has only a handful of ingredients and the result is such a treat. Follow a few key steps carefully and you will be making this scrumptious *pide* again and again.

7 g (¼ oz/1 sachet) instant dry yeast
185 ml (6 fl oz/¾ cup) warm water
1 teaspoon sugar
300 g (10½ oz/scant 2½ cups) plain (all-purpose) flour, plus extra for dusting
1 teaspoon sea salt
2 tablespoons salted butter, cubed, plus 1 tablespoon for the topping
3 medium eggs
1 teaspoon olive oil, plus extra for greasing
120 g (4 oz) medium Cheddar (or Trabzon's *kolot* cheese), grated
200 g (7 oz) mozzarella, grated

Combine the yeast, warm water and sugar in a small bowl. Mix well, cover and set aside for 15 minutes.

In a large mixing bowl, combine the flour and salt. Create a well in the middle and pour in the frothy yeast mixture. Knead with your hands for 2–3 minutes to bring the dough together. Place the dough onto a clean, dry, lightly floured surface. Add the cubed butter to the dough and knead well for another 2–3 minutes until you achieve a smooth dough ball. Lightly oil the mixing bowl, place the dough in, cover with cling film (plastic wrap) and a dish towel. Leave in a warm place to prove for 30 minutes.

After this period, punch back the dough and knead. Divide into two equal dough balls. Place them back into the bowl, cover and prove for another 30 minutes.

Preheat the oven to 200°C fan/220°C/ 425°F/gas 7. Line two baking sheets with baking paper.

Once the dough is risen, place one of the dough balls on a lightly floured surface, keeping the other covered. Stretch the dough into a thin, round shape, about 27 cm (11 in) in diameter. Place on a baking sheet. Repeat with the other dough and place on the other baking sheet.

Separate the whites of the eggs into a bowl, carefully placing the whole yolks on a plate nearby. Transfer one of the yolks to a small bowl and add the teaspoon of olive oil to this yolk and combine well.

Brush a 3 cm (1 in) band of egg white around the edges of both dough circles and fold in the dough edges to create a 2 cm (¾ in) border. Press well so that edges stick to the dough – the brushed egg white will help seal them. Brush the borders of both *pide* with the egg yolk mixture. Drizzle 1 tablespoon of water over the middle part of each dough and brush to cover the whole middle part (the water will prevent it puffing up). Bake both *pide* for 8 minutes until the edges are golden.

Remove from the oven and spread half of the Cheddar and half of the mozzarella on each *pide* evenly. Drizzle 2 tablespoons of water all round the middle part and dot over a few small dabs of butter. Bake for a further 7 minutes until the cheese is melted.

Remove from the oven and create a little dent in the middle of each *pide*. Carefully slide an egg yolk into each hollow. Bake for a final 1½–2 minutes, making sure the yolk is still runny. Serve immediately.

Ekmek, Börek, Pide

+ **Serving suggestion:** *Cevizli Bat Salatası* (page
  123) would be a wonderful accompaniment
  to this delicious *pide*.

Mısır Ekmeği

Corn Bread

Serves 6–8

Corn is a major staple in the Black Sea region and corn bread is vital and much loved in the area. There are a few versions of corn bread and this one comes from the Rize province. We tested many corn breads to achieve this *Mısır Ekmeği* (with sincere thanks to my dear friend Gülsüm Genç Koç, originally from Rize, a very talented baker herself and the owner of Mill Hill Artisan Bakery in London. Special thanks too to sevgili Emine Teyze, Gülsüm's mum, for her valuable tips). Locals simply enjoy it hot straight from the oven, spread with butter, with the region's creamy yoghurt or with soups, such as the Black Sea's much loved *Karalahana Çorbası* (collard green soup with borlotti beans and corn, page 84).

500 g (1 lb 2 oz/4 cups) fine cornmeal or maize flour (also known as corn flour, not cornflour/ cornstarch)
1 teaspoon bicarbonate of soda (baking soda)
1 teaspoon fresh lemon juice
7 g (¼ oz) sea salt
1 tablespoon vegetable oil, plus ½ teaspoon
85 g (3 oz) unsalted butter, melted
670 ml (23 fl oz/2¾ cups) hot water

Preheat the oven to 200°C fan/220°C/ 425°F/gas 7. Line a round or square baking dish, 20 cm (8 in) in diameter, with baking paper.

Combine the fine cornmeal or maize flour, bicarbonate of soda, lemon juice and salt in a large mixing bowl and mix well. Make a well in the middle and pour in the tablespoon of vegetable oil and the melted butter. Combine thoroughly with a large spoon.

Pour in a third of the hot water and combine well with a spoon until all the water is absorbed. Add another third of the hot water and combine as before. Add the remaining hot water and combine until you achieve a very soft, almost sliding off the spoon dough (depending on the flour used, you may need to add a little bit more hot water to achieve this consistency). Pour the mixture into the prepared dish.

Pour the ½ teaspoon oil into a bowl of warm water. Dampen your hands with the mixture and gently press the top of the dough to spread it evenly in the dish. This will help achieve a nice crust on top and keep the inside moist. Bake on the middle shelf of the oven for 55 minutes–1 hour, or until you achieve a nice darkish golden crust.

Take the corn bread out of the oven and turn it onto a large plate. Remove the baking paper and place the baking dish back over the top of the corn bread for 5 minutes to rest, so that the bread keeps moist. Slice and serve warm immediately, with butter spread over the top.

✦ **Tip:** You need to use hot water to make Turkish-style corn bread and make sure the maize flour/fine cornmeal absorbs the hot water before baking.

Kahvaltı

Two

All-Day Breakfast

Kahvaltı

For many Turks (including me), *kahvaltı* (a hearty breakfast) is our favourite meal of the day. I have such special memories of gathering around the breakfast table with my family to enjoy a leisurely Turkish breakfast, washed down with glasses of *çay* (Turkish tea). On special occasions, we would gather together with friends and family at one of our favourite cafés by the Bosphorus in Istanbul. With the boats passing by, the sun on our backs, and *çay* in our hands, we would delight in an unrushed Turkish breakfast — and, in my view, a perfect morning.

The options for a Turkish breakfast are heavenly. As the title suggests, the recipes in this chapter can be enjoyed at any time of the day, too. From herby *Kaygana* crêpes (page 58) to *Fırında Yumurtalı Sebzeli Ekmek* (baked bread with eggs and vegetables, page 56) to *Çılbır* (Turkish-style poached eggs over garlicky yoghurt, page 61), the recipes in this chapter are a taste sensation. *Patatesli Yumurta* (page 64) has a particularly special place in my heart as it was my father's favourite — at any opportunity he would turn leftover potatoes into this delicious and easy dish. Eggs take centre stage in Turkish breakfast. You will also find the delightful *Nar Eksili Zeytin Salatası* (olive salad with pomegranate molasses and walnuts, page 66) on our breakfast table, southern Turkish style. I hope you enjoy your *kahvaltı* feast all day long.

Fırında Yumurtalı Sebzeli Ekmek

Baked Bread with Egg and Vegetables

Serves 3–4

As a child, I loved the smell of the baked melted cheese happily married with the eggs and vegetables on bread, and I am still very fond of it; I can eat it anytime of the day. My mother would also make this and variations of it, using ingredients she had to hand, for *Suhoor* (the meal consumed early in the morning by Muslims before fasting during Ramadan). It is a delicious way to use up leftover bread, vegetables and cheese.

3 medium eggs
2 medium tomatoes, finely chopped
4 spring onions (scallions), trimmed and finely chopped
85 g (3 oz) medium Cheddar (or Turkish *kaşar peyniri***),** grated
110 g (3¾ oz) mozzarella, grated
small handful of fresh herbs (parsley, basil or coriander/cilantro), chopped
2 tablespoons olive oil
sea salt and freshly ground black pepper, to taste
4 chunky slices of bread

Preheat the oven to 180°C fan/200°C/400°F/gas 6. Line a baking sheet with non-stick baking paper.

Beat the eggs in a large bowl. Add the tomatoes, spring onions, grated cheeses, herbs and olive oil, season with salt and pepper, and mix well.

Place the slices of bread on the baking sheet. Spread the mixture evenly on each slice and bake in the oven for about 15 minutes until the topping starts to melt and turn golden.

+ **Variation:** Chopped up peppers, courgettes (zucchini) and mushrooms all work well here. You can use sliced olives instead of cheese. You can also omit the eggs and use a plant-based cheese for a vegan alternative.

+ **Serving suggestion:** Serve with *Kısır* (page 130) for a satisfying meal.

Kaygana

Crêpes with Parsley and Spring Onions

Makes 5

These fragrant, savoury crêpes are a popular breakfast, especially in the Black Sea region and the northeastern part of the country. It's a cross between an omelette and a Western-style crêpe and each region, almost each house, has their own version. In the Black Sea region chopped anchovy might be added; some may have it less eggy, some may add more herbs, garlic or spring onions (scallions). In the city of Trabzon, traditionally *kaygana* are made using water instead of milk.

255 ml (8½ fl oz/1 cup) full-fat milk
165 g (5½ oz/1⅓ cups) plain (all-purpose) flour
4 medium eggs, beaten
small handful of flat-leaf parsley, finely chopped
3 spring onions (scallions), trimmed and finely chopped
sea salt and freshly ground black pepper, to taste
2 tablespoons melted unsalted butter

Combine the milk and flour in a large mixing bowl and whisk until you reach a smooth consistency. Pour in the beaten eggs and whisk again until well combined. Stir in the chopped parsley and spring onions, season with salt and pepper and combine well.

Brush a wide, non-stick, 25 cm (10 in) frying pan (skillet) with the melted butter and heat over medium–high heat. Pour a ladle of the *kaygana* batter into the pan and swirl it around so the bottom of the pan is evenly coated in a thin layer. Cook over a high heat for about 45 seconds–1 minute on one side until golden. Use a wide spatula to flip the crêpe over and cook the other side for 30–45 seconds, until darkish golden blobs appear. Transfer to a serving plate.

Cook the rest of the *kaygana* this way, brushing the pan with melted butter each time. Roll the crêpes into individual rolls and place side by side on a serving plate.

✦ **Serving suggestions:** My family loves *kaygana* with jam; try my *Kuru İncir Reçeli* (dried fig jam, page 242) for a lovely accompaniment, with thin slices of mature Cheddar (or Turkish *kaşar* cheese) on the side if you like.

Çılbır

Turkish-Style Poached Eggs in Garlicky Yoghurt

Serves 2

(GF)

This is one of my favourite ways to enjoy eggs. It was part of Ottoman palace banquets and a favourite of Mehmed the Conqueror. At home, *Çılbır* is generally enjoyed as a hot *meze*; I also like serving it as part of a leisurely weekend breakfast, lunch or a light mid-week supper – a versatile dish.

1 large garlic clove
sea salt, to taste
400 g (14 oz/1⅔ cups)
  strained yoghurt
2 tablespoons apple cider,
  grape or white wine
  vinegar
2 large eggs
2 tablespoons olive oil
2 teaspoons *pul biber* or
  red pepper flakes

TO SERVE
1 teaspoon finely
  chopped dill or parsley
flatbreads or crusty bread
  (maybe *Balon Ekmek*,
  page 44)

Prepare the garlicky yoghurt about 30 minutes before poaching the eggs, to bring to room temperature. Finely chop the garlic and sprinkle over a pinch of salt. Using the flat side of the knife, gently squash the garlic to turn it into a fine paste. In a small bowl, beat the yoghurt with the garlic, then spoon onto two serving plates, creating a round thick layer to provide a nest for the poached egg.

Fill a small pan with hot water, add a pinch of salt and the vinegar (this will help to seal the egg whites) and bring to the boil. Stir the water to create a whirlpool and crack in the first egg. As the egg spins and the white sets around the yolk, stir the water ready for the next one. Poach each egg for 2–3 minutes so that the yolk remains soft.

While the eggs are poaching, quickly pour in the olive oil into a small pan and stir in the *pul biber*. Stir to gently infuse the oil for 30 seconds over a low–medium heat, then remove from the heat.

Lift the poached eggs out of the water with a slotted spoon and place them on a couple of sturdy paper towels to absorb any excess moisture, then gently place them on the garlic yoghurt. Drizzle the infused olive oil over the poached eggs and season with salt to taste. Scatter with chopped dill or parsley and serve immediately with bread, if you like.

Bayat Ekmekli, Sebzeli Yumurta

Unscrambled Menemen with Leftover Bread

Serves 3

I love *menemen*, our iconic Turkish scrambled eggs with vegetables. Though I must say, I equally adore this unscrambled version. My mother would add stale chunks of bread to the pan, to liven up the bread and soak up all the delicious flavours, something I highly recommend. It is a scrumptious all-in-one-pan dish that I can eat all day.

3 tablespoons olive oil
1 medium onion, finely chopped
1 green (bell) pepper or 2 pointy green *sivri biber*, deseeded and finely chopped
3 ripe medium tomatoes, finely chopped
4 spring onions (scallions), trimmed and finely chopped
small bunch of flat-leaf parsley, finely chopped (reserve 1 teaspoon for serving)
sea salt and freshly ground black pepper
3 medium eggs
60 g (2 oz) crumbled *beyaz peynir* or feta
pinch each of ground cumin and *pul biber*
110 g (3¾ oz) chunks of stale bread

Heat the olive oil in a wide pan over a medium–high heat, add the onion and sauté for 8 minutes until starting to caramelise around the edges. Stir in the peppers and sauté for 3 minutes, then add the tomatoes and spring onions and cook for a further 3 minutes. Stir in the parsley and season with salt and pepper.

Create three holes in the sauce mixture and carefully crack in your eggs. Crumble the cheese around the sauce and egg whites, and sprinkle a pinch of cumin and *pul biber* over the egg yolks. Gently place the chunks of bread around the sauce. Cook over a medium heat for 4–5 minutes until the egg whites are set but the yolks are still runny, turning the bread pieces once to soften and soak up the juices.

Serve immediately, with the reserved chopped parsley scattered over.

✦ **Serving suggestion:** For a bigger feast, combine with *Tahinli Fasulye Piyazı* (page 120).

Patatesli Yumurta

Sautéed Potatoes with Spring Onion and Eggs

Serves 2

This delicious dish was among my dear belated father Orhan's favourites. My dear mother, Gülçin, was an amazing cook, who loved to feed anyone around – my ultimate source of inspiration. She was also a busy science teacher, so whenever she was on late duty at school my father would knock this up for supper with a big smile on his face. I am my father's daughter and absolutely adore this delicious, warming comfort food. Pungent ground cumin is the star spice here and goes so well with potato and eggs.

255 g (9 oz) potatoes (Maris Piper work well)
sea salt and freshly ground black pepper, to taste
3 tablespoons olive oil
½ teaspoon ground cumin
¼ teaspoon *pul biber* (add more if you like)
3 spring onions (scallions), trimmed and finely chopped
2 medium eggs
40 g (1½ oz) *beyaz peynir*, feta or cheese of your choice, crumbled
a few sprigs of flat-leaf parsley, finely chopped

Wash and pat dry the potatoes, then cut into 2.5 cm (1 in) cubes, keeping the skin on. Place in a medium saucepan, cover with plenty of hot water, add a pinch of salt and bring to the boil. Partially cover and cook over a medium heat for 15 minutes until the potatoes are cooked but still firm. Drain well.

Heat the olive oil in a wide, non-stick pan over a medium heat, add the potatoes, season with salt and sauté for 8 minutes. Add the cumin and *pul biber* and sauté for a further 2 minutes, stirring often, until the potatoes turn golden. Stir in the spring onions and combine well. Create two hollows in the pan and crack the eggs. Sprinkle the crumbled cheese over the potatoes and egg white and cook for about 4 minutes until the egg whites are set and the yolks still runny. Season with a little more salt and pepper if you like. Sprinkle over the chopped parsley and serve immediately.

+ **Serving suggestion:** I suggest serving with *Cevizli Bat Salatası* (page 123) to make this a substantial meal.

Nar Ekşili Zeytin Salatası

Olive Salad with Pomegranate Molasses and Walnuts

Serves 4-6

Olives (*zeytin*) are a big part of the Turkish diet, a must at the breakfast table, and included in savoury pastries and bakes as well as in salads. I had this salad during a visit to my hometown Antakya in 2022 at the wonderful Meriç Farm, *Meriç Çiftliği*. The owners, the very hospitable Serra and Hadice Nalçabasmaz, prepared us a beautiful spread, including this delicious olive salad, fresh from their olive harvest. It features the region's much loved tangy pomegranate molasses, *nar ekşisi*, and delightful crunchy walnuts, juicy peppers and sundried tomatoes. Pomegranate molasses is widely available these days, although you can make it with my recipe on page 220.

85 g (3 oz) **sundried tomatoes,** finely diced

3 **spring onions (scallions),** trimmed and finely chopped

1 **red pointy or bell pepper,** deseeded and diced

55 g (2 oz) **shelled walnuts,** finely chopped

110 g (3¾ oz) **Turkish or other good-quality pitted green and black olives,** roughly chopped

small handful of flat-leaf parsley, finely chopped

sea salt and freshly ground black pepper, to taste

FOR THE DRESSING

1 **tablespoon pomegranate molasses** (*nar ekşisi,* see page 220 for homemade)

2 **tablespoons extra-virgin olive oil**

½ **teaspoon ground cumin**

Combine all the salad ingredients except the parsley and seasoning in a large bowl.

In a small bowl, mix the dressing ingredients and pour over the salad.

Season with salt and freshly ground black pepper and combine well. Add the parsley and gently give everything a good mix, ready to serve.

+ **Prepare ahead and variation:** You can prepare this a day ahead and keep covered in the refrigerator. You could also add ½ teaspoon fragrant za'atar (available in most supermarkets) to the dressing for a lovely variation.

+ **Serving suggestions:** Enjoy as part of breakfast, lunch, as *meze,* in wraps, or with savoury pastries such as *Patatesli, Ispanaklı Gözleme* (page 170). Leftovers are fantastic combined with pasta, rice or bulgur, too.

Muhlama / Kuymak

Melted Cheese and Cornmeal/Maize Flour with Butter

Serves 6-8

This rich combination of maize flour, made by grinding dried whole corn kernels (also known as corn flour in the US and not to be confused with cornflour/cornstarch), butter and oozing melting cheese, is known as *Muhlama* or *Kuymak* and is a real Black Sea specialty. Almost every city in the Black Sea region has their own variation. It is also popular in the neighbouring Azerbaijan and Georgia. Made with the region's delicious creamy butter and melting local *çeçil* or *kolot* cheese, it is the ultimate Black-Sea-style breakfast, traditionally cooked in a *sahan* (copper pan). I had the pleasure of enjoying the real thing at the very scenic Isgobya Dağ Evleri in Maçka, near Trabzon, made by the very hospitable Leyla Hanım. Overlooking the majestic landscape near Sümela monastery, it was an unforgettable, indulgent experience.

85 g (3 oz) **unsalted butter,** cubed

85 g (3 oz/⅔ cup) **fine cornmeal or maize flour** (also known as corn flour – not cornflour/ cornstarch)

655 ml (22 fl oz/2¾ cups) **water**

sea salt, to taste

250 g (9 oz) **melting cheese** (*dil peyniri,* mild Cheddar, mozzarella or any stringy cheese), grated

TO SERVE

45 g (1¾ oz) **unsalted butter**

Mısır Ekmeği (page 50) or flatbreads

Melt the cubed butter in a 25 cm (10 in) pan over a medium heat. Once the butter starts to bubble, add the cornmeal or maize flour and cook, stirring for 2–3 minutes until the flour is slightly darker in colour. Add the water, season with salt and cook, stirring often, for 4–5 minutes over a medium–high heat until the flour has absorbed most of the water. The mixture will have a pudding-like pourable consistency. Stir in the cheese and combine well. Keep stirring for 1–2 minutes over a medium heat until the cheese is melted, stringy and oozy.

Meanwhile, heat the butter for serving in a small pan until bubbly. Pour the melted butter over the cheesy *muhlama* and combine well for a minute. Serve immediately from the pan – it needs to stay hot to be oozy – with bread for dipping.

+ **Serving suggestion:** *Muhlama* is rich and a little goes a long way. Locals enjoy it with the region's *Mısır Ekmeği* (Corn Bread, page 50) dipped straight into the *muhlama* pan. This recipe makes a generous portion; leftovers can be kept in the refrigerator, covered, and reheated the next day.

Nergisleme

Egg Salad with Spring Onion and Herbs

Serves 4-6

Nergisleme is a lovely, refreshing salad, especially enjoyed in the southeast. It is traditionally made to welcome spring, when the first spring onions (scallions) come out. It takes its name from the spring flower narcissus or daffodil (*nergis* in Turkish), as it shares similar colours. It is particularly enjoyed during the Nevruz celebrations (also known as the Parsi New Year, celebrated in many countries on the Silk Road, and especially in the southeastern region of *Türkiye*/Turkey), when locals pick narcissi from the fields to decorate their table.

6 medium eggs
6 spring onions
  (scallions), trimmed and
  finely sliced (including the
  green stems)
45 g (1 ¾ oz/a large bunch)
  flat-leaf parsley, finely
  chopped (including the
  stems)
15 g (½ oz) fresh mint
  leaves, finely chopped

FOR THE DRESSING
2 tablespoons extra-
  virgin olive oil, plus extra
  to serve
1 tablespoon fresh lemon
  juice
sea salt and freshly ground
  black pepper, to taste

TO SERVE
½ teaspoon ground
  cumin
½ teaspoon *pul biber*
Balon Ekmek (page 44) or
  flatbreads

Place the whole eggs in a medium saucepan and add enough cold water to cover by 1 cm (½ in). Bring to the boil, then simmer for 10–11 minutes. Drain and cool the eggs under cold running water for a minute (this helps prevent dark rings forming between the egg white and the yolk and assists with peeling). Peel the eggs and set aside.

Combine the spring onions, parsley and mint in a mixing bowl.

In a separate bowl, combine the olive oil and lemon juice, and season with salt and pepper. Pour the dressing over the salad and mix well. Transfer to a serving plate.

Quarter each egg lengthways and scatter over the salad. Drizzle with a little extra-virgin olive oil and sprinkle with cumin and *pul biber*. Season to taste and serve with flatbreads.

✦ **Variation:** Though not traditional, you can add cubed boiled potato (about 85 g/3 oz – great for using up leftover potatoes) for a more substantial meal, in which case you may need to adjust the seasoning and drizzle with a little more extra-virgin olive oil.

Çorba

Three

Soups

Çorba

S oups have a special place in Turkish cuisine. Traditionally, Turkish meals start with a bowl of *çorba* (soup) followed by *meze*. Sometimes soup is enjoyed for breakfast, such as *Ezo Gelin Çorbası* (page 83) for a hearty start to the day in rural Anatolia. Turkish soups are wholesome, delicious and great value, using store-cupboard ingredients, seasonal produce, grains and legumes. They offer great, balanced choices for vegetarian and vegan diets. They are satisfying, too, and in my house they can very easily be the main event.

There is a variety of Turkish soups from different regions on offer in this chapter, which you can prepare ahead and freeze. My family loves *Pazılı Lebeniye Çorbası* (yoghurt soup with chickpeas and Swiss chard, page 74) served with their favourite *Ispanaklı Gül Böreği* (page 38) for a satisfying supper. Hearty *Karalahana Çorbası* (page 84) is another specialty from the Black Sea region that I would love you to try. It is a taste sensation with earthy borlotti beans, the sweetness of the corn, slightly bitter greens and a lovely kick from a *pul biber* sauce. As you will notice, in Turkish soups a spice-infused melted butter or olive oil is often poured over the top for an irresistible extra layer of flavour.

Pazılı Lebeniye Çorbası

Yoghurt Soup with Chickpeas and Swiss Chard

Serves 4–6

This delicious, wholesome soup is inspired by Gaziantep's *Lebeniye* soup. Traditionally, minced (ground) meat is added and locals tend to make the soup in the spring, when the chard (*pazı*) first comes out. Locals use the stalks in the soup and save the chard leaves to make other dishes, such as stuffed leaves with rice and herbs (*sarma*). I chose to use the chard as a whole here; I adore its savoury taste and it works so well with yoghurt and infused oil.

2 tablespoons olive oil
4 garlic cloves, finely chopped
200 g (7 oz) Swiss chard, trimmed and finely chopped, including stems
115 g (4 oz/generous ½ cup) long-grain rice, rinsed
225 g (8 oz/1½ cups) pre-cooked, rinsed chickpeas (garbanzo beans) (discard any loose skins)
1.1 litres (37 fl oz/scant 4½ cups) hot water
sea salt and freshly ground black pepper, to taste
650 g (1 lb 7 oz/scant 2½ cups) strained (*süzme*) whole milk yoghurt
1 medium egg, beaten

FOR THE INFUSED OIL
2 tablespoons olive oil
1 teaspoon dried mint
1 teaspoon *pul biber*

Heat the oil in a medium–large saucepan over a medium heat, add the garlic and sauté for 1–2 minutes. Add the chopped chard and sauté for another 2 minutes, then stir in the rice and chickpeas, and pour in the hot water. Season with salt and pepper, combine well, and bring to the boil, then cover and cook over a medium–low heat for 15 minutes, stirring occasionally.

Place the strained yoghurt in a large bowl, add the beaten egg and combine. Take 1 ladle of hot water from the pan and slowly blend into the yoghurt and egg mixture, then add another ladle of hot water to the mixture and combine well. This will help to bring the yoghurt mixture to the soup temperature gently and avoid curdling. Pour this mixture into the soup and carefully combine, then bring to a gentle simmer over a low–medium heat, stirring constantly. Simmer for a further 3–4 minutes over a low heat, season to taste, then remove from the heat.

FOR THE INFUSED OIL, pour the olive oil into a small sauté pan, stir in the dried mint and *pul biber,* and stir gently over a low heat (so that the spices don't burn) for about 30 seconds to infuse.

Pour the infused oil into the soup and combine well. Serve immediately while warm.

+ **Serving suggestion:** You could serve this delicious soup with *Ispanaklı Katıklı Ekmek* (page 46) for a satisfying meal.

Balkabaklı Kestane Çorbası

Pumpkin and Chestnut Soup

Serves 4

Pumpkin (*balkabağı*) is enjoyed in savoury and sweet dishes at home. While it can be combined with yoghurt or with pomegranate molasses in the south for savoury meals (for example, *Adesiye*, page 143), it is cooked with chestnuts in the north. The city of Zonguldak in the Black Sea region grows some of the finest chestnuts and this soup is a Zonguldak specialty. The sweetness of the pumpkin and onions works beautifully with the earthy chestnuts. Locals would also add the region's creamy *manda sütü* (water buffalo's milk) to the soup – full-fat milk works well as a substitute although you can use single (light) cream for a creamier taste. You can use butternut squash instead of pumpkin, too.

2 tablespoons olive oil or sunflower oil
2 medium onions, finely chopped
825 g (1 lb 13 oz) deseeded and peeled pumpkin, sliced into 1 cm (½ in) chunks
255 g (9 oz) peeled, cooked chestnuts, quartered
510 ml (18 fl oz/generous 2 cups) vegetable stock
510 ml (18 fl oz/generous 2 cups) water
sea salt and freshly ground black pepper, to taste
140 ml (5 fl oz/scant ⅔ cup) full-fat milk (or a plant-based alternative)
handful of fresh parsley, chopped, to serve

FOR THE SAUTÉED CHESTNUTS
2 tablespoons olive oil or sunflower oil
80 g (3 oz) peeled, cooked chestnuts, diced into small bites

Heat the oil in a large, heavy saucepan over a medium heat, add the onions and sauté for 10 minutes until softened. Stir in the pumpkin pieces and sauté for another 2 minutes. Add the chestnuts, pour in the vegetable stock and water, then season with salt and pepper, and combine well. Bring to the boil, then simmer for 12–15 minutes until the pumpkin is cooked.

Purée the soup in a blender and pour back into the pan, add the milk and bring back to the boil, then simmer for 5 minutes. Seasoning is important – check and add more salt and pepper to your taste.

FOR THE SAUTÉED CHESTNUTS, heat the oil in a small sauté pan over a medium heat, add the chestnuts and sauté for 3 minutes. Season with salt and pepper.

Serve the soup warm with the sautéed chestnuts and chopped parsley sprinkled over.

+ **Serving suggestion:** Serve with *Mısır Ekmeği* (page 50) to complement this delicious soup.

Çorba

Terbiyeli Sebze Çorbası

Vegetable Soup with Egg and Lemon Sauce

Serves 4–6

In Anatolia, most folks start the day with a bowl of hearty soup. We have a variety of nutritious, delicious soups and this one uses the *terbiyeli* technique, which involves beating lemon juice with the egg yolks to thicken the soup and to create a delicious sort of tangy flavour, which I love. This method requires a staged tempering of the egg sauce into the hot liquid so that the soup doesn't curdle. It's a chunky, satisfying soup, a meal in itself, and a great way to use up any vegetables you have to hand – beetroot, sweet potatoes, courgettes (zucchini) and peas would all work well here.

2 tablespoons olive oil
1 large or 2 medium
  onions, finely chopped
400 g (14 oz) potatoes,
  diced into 1 cm (½ in)
  cubes
280 g (10 oz) carrots,
  trimmed and cut into 1 cm
  (½ in) cubes
250 g (9 oz) celery sticks,
  cut into 1 cm (½ in) chunks
sea salt and freshly ground
  black pepper
1.2 litres (40 fl oz/4¾ cups)
  hot water
85 g (3 oz) orzo pasta (or
  gluten-free small pasta
  or rice)
2 egg yolks, beaten
juice of 1 lemon
1 teaspoon *pul biber*
small bunch of parsley,
  finely chopped
lemon wedges, to serve

Heat the olive oil in a large saucepan over a medium–high heat, add the onions and sauté for 5 minutes. Stir in the potato, carrots and celery, season with salt and pepper, and sauté for 2 minutes. Add the hot water, cover and bring to the boil, then reduce the heat to low and simmer for 25 minutes, covered.

Add the orzo to the pan and cook for a further 10 minutes, stirring occasionally.

Meanwhile, combine the beaten egg yolks with the lemon juice in a small bowl. Gently pour a ladle of the soup liquid into the egg mixture and blend well. Slowly pour the sauce into the simmering soup pot, stirring constantly so that the eggs don't curdle. Cook very gently over a low heat for 3–5 minutes. Do not allow the soup to boil, or it may curdle. Check the seasoning and stir in the *pul biber*, then remove from the heat.

Add the chopped parsley, give it a good stir and serve immediately, with wedges of lemon on the side. The soup thickens as it sits, so you may like to add a little more water if served later.

Erişteli Yesil Mercimek Çorbası

Green Lentil and Egg Noodle Soup

Serves 4-6

Erişte, a type of egg noodle, is enjoyed throughout the southern and eastern part of the country with variations. It is widely prepared in Anatolia in the summer months, cut, dried and stored in muslin bags to be used in winter. Making and drying noodles is an ancient preservation technique practiced in Central Asia and in countries along the Silk Road for thousands of years. This green lentil and *erişte* noodle soup is a delicious one-pot winter warmer, as my husband says. Please don't skip the fragrant dried mint and *pul biber* infused oil, as it really elevates the soup's taste with a nice heat and refreshing flavour.

**FOR THE ERIŞTE DOUGH
(MAKES 360 G/13 OZ EGG NOODLES)**

270 g (10 oz/generous 2 cups) **plain (all-purpose) flour,** plus extra for dusting

⅓ teaspoon **sea salt**

1 medium **egg**

100 ml (3½ fl oz/scant ½ cup) **lukewarm water**

FOR THE SOUP

200 g (7 oz/generous 1 cup) **green lentils,** rinsed

2 tablespoons **butter or olive oil**

2 medium **onions,** finely chopped

60 g (2 oz/¼ cup) **double concentrated tomato paste**

1.275 litres (45 fl oz/5 cups) **hot water**

salt and freshly ground black pepper

200 g (7 oz) *erişte* **noodles or fresh tagliatelle**

FOR THE INFUSED OIL

3 tablespoons **olive oil or melted butter**

1 tablespoon **dried mint**

2 teaspoons *pul biber* **(or more, if you enjoy heat)**

First, make the *erişte* dough. Sift the flour into a large mixing bowl, sprinkle with the salt and make a well in the middle. Crack the egg into the well and use your hands to mix, pulling the flour in from the sides. Slowly add the water, 2 tablespoons at a time, combining well. Once all the water has been added, knead the mixture into a firm, quite hard dough. Turn onto a lightly floured surface and knead for 3–4 minutes (add a little extra flour if it is sticky) until you achieve a smooth, firm dough. Place the dough in a bowl, cover with a damp kitchen cloth and leave to rest for 25 minutes.

Once the dough is rested, place on a lightly floured surface and divide into three equal balls. Use a rolling pin to roll each out to a 23 cm (9 in) circle.

Gently warm a dry 25 cm (10 in) non-stick pan over a low heat. Place one of the dough circles on the pan and dry it out, turning the dough over every 10–15 seconds with a fish slice (so it won't cook), for about 3 minutes until dried out. Take care that it doesn't harden completely; the dough circle should still be able to gently bend. Place on a dry tray to cool and repeat the procedure for the remaining two dough circles.

Cut each dough circle into quarters and then into 6 cm (½ in) strips, 1 cm (½ in) wide. Lay a clean, dry cloth on a table and spread the *erişte* noodles over

it in one layer. Let dry completely for 2–3 hours.

FOR THE SOUP, put the lentils into a large pan, add enough hot water to cover the lentils by 4 cm (1½ in), partially cover and simmer for 13 minutes. Drain and set the lentils aside.

Heat the butter or olive oil in the same pan over a medium–high heat, add the onions and sauté for 10 minutes until softened and starting to caramelise. Stir in the tomato paste and lentils, combining well. Add the measured hot water, season with salt and pepper, partially cover and cook for 8–10 minutes over a medium–low heat, gently bubbling. Stir in the *erişte* noodles and cook for a further 10–11 minutes until the *erişte* is cooked and the soup thickened. The soup will thicken further as it sits, so you may need to add a little more water, making sure it is still a chunky soup. Remove from the heat.

FOR THE INFUSED OIL, heat the butter or olive oil in a small pan, stir in the dried mint and *pul biber*, and gently infuse over a low heat, stirring often, for 30 seconds.

Serve the soup hot, poured into bowls, with a spoonful of the infused oil drizzled over. Sprinkle over a little more *pul biber*, if you enjoy heat.

+ **Prepare ahead:** *Erişte* can be made ahead of time. Once cut and completely dried, *erişte* can be stored in a clean muslin bag in a dry, cool place away from sunshine for 1-2 months.

+ **Quick variation:** If pressed for time, use fresh tagliatelle pasta cut into 6 cm (½ in) strips instead. Stir into the soup for the last 5 minutes of cooking time.

Ezo Gelin Çorbası

Spicy Bulgur and Lentil Soup

Serves 4-6

I couldn't leave out one of my (and most probably the nation's) favourite soups, *Ezo Gelin Çorbası*, as it is not only delicious but also a perfect example of vegetarian Turkish cuisine – easy, nutritious, great value, made with wholesome store-cupboard ingredients and flavoured naturally with spices and lemon juice. This hearty, chunky soup uses a southern Turkish condiment, pepper paste (*biber salçası*), which adds oodles of flavour. Although *biber salçası* is more widely available these days, you may enjoy making your own with my recipe on page 218.

2 tablespoons olive oil
1 medium onion, finely chopped
285 g (10 oz/generous 1 cup) split red lentils, rinsed and drained
1.75 litres (59 fl oz/7 cups) hot water
45 g (1¾ oz/¼ cup) coarse bulgur wheat, rinsed and drained
60 g (2 oz/¼ cup) double concentrated tomato paste
40 g (1½ oz/3 tablespoons) (sweet or hot) Turkish red pepper paste (*biber salçası*, see page 218 for homemade)
1 tablespoon dried mint
sea salt and freshly ground black pepper, to taste
juice of 1 lemon
lemon wedges, to serve

FOR THE INFUSED OIL
3 tablespoons olive oil
2 teaspoons dried mint
1 teaspoon *pul biber*

Heat the olive oil in a heavy, medium saucepan over a medium heat, add the onion and cook for 3-4 minutes, stirring often. Add the lentils and measured hot water, partially cover and bring to the boil. Cook over a medium-low heat for about 25 minutes, stirring occasionally. Skim off any foam formed at the top with a spoon.

Stir in the bulgur, tomato paste, red pepper paste and dried mint, season with salt and pepper, and combine well. Cover and cook for a further 10-15 minutes until the bulgur is cooked. Add some more water if the soup appears to be too thick. Pour in the lemon juice, adjust the seasoning to your taste and mix well.

FOR THE INFUSED OIL, heat the olive oil in a small pan, stir in the dried mint and *pul biber*, and gently infuse over a low heat, stirring often, for 30-40 seconds.

Pour the infused oil into the soup and combine well. Serve hot with lemon wedges on the side.

+ **Gluten-free option:** You can use quinoa instead of bulgur to make this soup gluten-free. In this case, cook the quinoa for 15 minutes when combined in the soup.

Karalahana Çorbası
Collard Greens Soup with Borlotti Beans and Sweetcorn

Serves 6 generously

Hearty *Karalahana Çorbası* encapsulates the staple ingredients in Black Sea cuisine, with many variations within the region. This version is inspired by my travels; I was served it at Sümer restaurant on the way to Maçka, near Trabzon. Made with the region's delicious butter, the sweetness of the corn is a delightful match to the slightly bitter greens (*karalahana*). You can enjoy this chunky, good-value soup with *Mısır Ekmeği* (page 50) as the locals do.

170 g (6 oz/generous ¾ cup) dried borlotti beans

2 tablespoons melted butter (or olive oil for a vegan option)

2 medium onions, finely chopped

85 g (3 oz/⅓ cup) double concentrated tomato paste

225 g (8 oz/generous 1 cup) sweetcorn kernels (cut from 2 medium cobs)

225 g (8 oz) collard greens, washed, rough stems removed and coarsely chopped

1.475 litres (52 fl oz/6 cups) hot water

sea salt and freshly ground black pepper, to taste

30 g (1 oz/¼ cup) fine cornmeal or maize flour (also known as corn flour – not cornflour/cornstarch)

FOR THE PUL BIBER SAUCE

3 tablespoons melted butter (or olive oil)

1 tablespoon *pul biber* (use less or more to your taste)

Soak the dried borlotti beans overnight or for 8 hours in plenty of cold water.

The next day, drain the beans, place in a large saucepan and cover with hot water. Bring to the boil, then cook over a medium heat for 20 minutes. Stir often and skim off any foam forming on the top with a spoon. Drain in a colander and refresh under cold running water (to retain colour and texture) and set aside in a bowl. They will be partially cooked and still firm, with a bite to them.

Heat the butter (or olive oil) in a large pan over a medium–high heat, add the onions and sauté for 7 minutes, stirring often to soften. Stir in the tomato paste, sweetcorn and the beans, and combine well. Add the collard greens and the measured hot water and bring to the boil. Gently mix – the collard greens will start to wilt. Season with salt and pepper, then cover, reduce the heat to medium–low and cook for 15 minutes, gently mixing a few times.

Place the fine cornmeal/maize flour in a small bowl and add 3 ladlefuls of the soup liquid. Mix with a spoon until the flour is dissolved and the mixture smooth. Pour into the pan and gently combine well. Cover and simmer for a further 10 minutes. This is a chunky soup but if it appears to be too thick for you, add a little more water and combine well.

FOR THE SAUCE, heat the butter (or olive oil) in a small pan and stir in the *pul biber*. Gently infuse for 30–45 seconds over a low heat.

Pour the *pul biber* sauce over the soup and check the seasoning. Serve immediately while hot.

+ **Prepare ahead:** You can make this ahead of time – the flavours settle and taste even better the next day.

+ **Quicker option:** This soup is best made with dried borlotti beans. If pressed for time, you can use 2 x 400 g (14 oz) cans of good-quality, pre-cooked and rinsed beans instead. Fold the beans into the soup before adding the maize/corn flour to the pot.

Meze

Four

Meze, as they are known in *Türkiye* (Turkey), are small, flavourful dishes that have an important place in everyday meals throughout the country. Originating from the Persian word *mazzeh*, which means 'pleasant taste' or 'snack', *meze* were designed to whet the appetite before moving onto the main course. Our *meze* can typically be yoghurt-, vegetable-, nut- or pulse-based and vary throughout different regions at home. For instance, spices and pepper paste are used liberally in the south, such as in *Muhammara* (page 97), while *Kırmızı Biberli Fava* (page 94) showcases the lighter flavours of the Aegean.

I love the sharing element of a *meze* feast, and a combination of just a couple of *meze* dishes served with flatbreads or savoury pastries can easily make a main meal for us. They can be conveniently prepared ahead of time, too. There is something for everyone in this chapter and I encourage you to experiment to create your *meze* feast. I absolutely adore *Nar Ekşili, Cevizli Pancar* (page 92) for instance – the sweetness of baked beets are fantastic combined with tangy pomegranate molasses and walnuts. How about having a go at crispy *Öcce* fritters (page 110)? They are not only delicious, but versatile, too. Leftovers of most of our *meze* can also be repurposed into another meal, as in Turkish *Şakşuka* (page 108); try combining *Şakşuka* leftovers with pasta, bulgur or rice, or crack eggs over for another satisfying meal.

Nar Ekşili, Cevizli Pancar

Beetroot with Walnuts and Pomegranate Molasses

Serves 4

We love beetroot (beets), or *pancar* as we call it in Turkish, and this baked beetroot with pomegranate molasses and walnuts is one of my favourite recipes in this book. Baking the beets brings out their natural sweetness and tastes fantastic combined with the tangy pomegranate molasses (*nar ekşisi*) and crunchy walnuts.

880 g (1 lb 15 oz) beetroot (beets)
2 tablespoons olive oil
sea salt and freshly ground black pepper, to taste
3 garlic cloves, finely chopped
2 tablespoons pomegranate molasses (*nar ekşisi*, see page 220 for homemade)
45 g (1¾ oz/⅓ cup) walnuts, chopped
handful of flat-leaf parsley, finely chopped
2 tablespoons pomegranate seeds

Preheat the oven to 180°C fan/200°C/400°F/gas 6.

Trim and peel the beetroot and slice into quarters lengthways. Slice each quarter into even bite-size chunks (about 1 cm/½ in). Place on a large baking tray, drizzle over the olive oil and season with salt and pepper. Use your hands to combine well (your hands will be stained but it's worth it to infuse the flavours – you can rub sliced lemon over your hands to get rid of the worst of the stain). Spread in one layer and bake for 30 minutes, turning them around halfway.

Remove the tray from the oven and stir in the chopped garlic. Bake for a further 6–7 minutes until the beets are cooked and starting to caramelise at the edges, taking care not to burn the garlic. Leave to cool for 5 minutes.

Transfer the beets to a serving bowl, drizzle over the pomegranate molasses and combine well. Add the chopped walnuts and parsley, and mix well. Decorate with pomegranate seeds just before serving.

+ **Prepare ahead:** This dish keeps well in the refrigerator for two to three days and leftovers can be enjoyed in multiple ways. If pressed for time, you can use ready-cooked beets, too, although you won't get the sweetness that baking them brings.

+ **Serving suggestions:** Combine with *Tahinli Fasulye Piyazı* (page 120) and *Kaygana* (page 58) for a substantial meal. Leftovers make a wonderful topping for *Kumpir* (page 166) and can also be used in *Pancarlı Nar Ekşili, Firik* (page 185).

Kırmızı Biberli Fava

Puréed Broad Beans with Dill and Sautéed Peppers

Serves 4

Fava is a popular *meze*, especially in Istanbul and the Aegean region. Traditionally, dried beans are used in this *meze* and, when in season, fresh broad (fava) beans can also be included. I use frozen beans as they are widely available. I absolutely love the earthy flavour of broad beans combined with lemon juice, dill and olive oil. This is not only a scrumptious *meze*, but also fantastic over toasted bread for lunch and dinner, too. This recipe is inspired by one of my favourite food writers, Ghillie Başan's version, where she uses tomatoes in the garnish.

500 g (1 lb 2 oz) frozen or fresh broad (fava) beans
2 tablespoons olive oil
1 medium onion, finely chopped
3 tablespoons extra-virgin olive oil
1 teaspoon finely chopped fresh dill, hard stalks removed (reserve a little for garnish)
2 tablespoons fresh lemon juice
¼ teaspoon brown sugar
sea salt, to taste

FOR THE SAUTÉED PEPPERS
2 tablespoons olive oil
1 red (bell) pepper, deseeded and diced
2 garlic cloves, finely chopped

If using frozen beans, place in a medium pan and simmer gently in lightly salted water for about 4 minutes, or until tender. If using fresh beans, simmer the podded beans in a pan of boiling water for 2 minutes. Drain and refresh under cold running water, then leave to cool in a bowl. When cool enough to handle, gently separate the outer shells with your fingers to pop out the bright green beans inside and place in a bowl – this is a little time consuming but well worth the effort for the best texture and flavour.

Heat the olive oil in a wide pan over a medium–high heat, add the onion and sauté for 5 minutes, stirring often until softened. Remove from the heat.

Place the prepared broad beans, sautéed onions and 2 tablespoons of the extra-virgin olive oil in a food processor and purée until smooth. Transfer to a medium bowl and stir in the dill, lemon juice, brown sugar,

remaining tablespoon of extra-virgin olive oil and season with salt to your taste. Combine well. If you like your *fava* set in moulds, as served in Istanbul, grease the base and sides of a small bowl with a little olive oil and fill the bowl with the mixture. Gently smooth the top, cover and rest in the refrigerator for 1–1½ hours to set.

FOR THE SAUTÉED PEPPERS, heat the olive oil in a pan over a medium–high heat, add the pepper and sauté for 5 minutes, stirring often. Add the garlic, season with salt and sauté for a further 2 minutes. Remove from the heat, stir in the reserved dill and set aside to cool.

When ready to eat, unmould the set *fava* onto a serving plate. Sprinkle the sautéed peppers around and a little over the top and drizzle with any remaining oil. Serve cold or at room temperature.

+ **If using dried beans:** Place 200 g (7 oz) dried broad (fava) beans in a bowl of cold water and soak overnight or for at least 6 hours. Drain and rinse, transfer to a pan and cover with water. Gently boil for 10 minutes, then simmer for 30 minutes, partially covered, or until fully cooked. Drain and set aside to use in the recipe.

+ **Prepare ahead:** *Fava* is fantastic to make a day or two ahead – keep in the refrigerator, covered.

+ **Serving suggestions:** Enjoy as part of a *meze* feast. Serve with *Çılbır* (page 61) for a delicious lunch or light supper.

Meze

Muhammara / Cevizli Biber

Walnut and Red Pepper Paste Dip

Serves 6-8

Muhammara, or *Cevizli Biber* as we call it in Antakya, is our favourite dip and is also enjoyed throughout the Middle East with variations. It is one of my mother's signature recipes and this version comes from her historic hometown, Antakya (ancient Antioch), and has been a part of every family get together. Whenever I make it abroad, I feel I am back home. It is easy to make and has a deliciously nutty flavour that makes you want to come back for more.

70 g (2½ oz) white or wholemeal stale bread (use gluten-free bread if you wish)
185 g (6½ oz) shelled walnuts
¼ small onion, finely chopped
3 tablespoons Turkish red pepper paste (*biber salçası*, see page 218 for homemade)
1 tablespoon double concentrated tomato paste
2 teaspoons ground cumin
sea salt, to taste
4 tablespoons extra-virgin olive oil, plus extra to serve
2 tablespoons water
pinch of *pul biber* or red pepper flakes
flatbreads or crackers, to serve

Soak the bread in water in a small bowl.

Blitz the walnuts, onion, red pepper and tomato pastes, cumin and a pinch of salt in a food processor. Squeeze the excess water out of the bread and crumble it into the food processor, add the extra-virgin olive oil and water, and blitz to a smooth spread. If it appears to be too thick, add a little more olive oil. Check the seasoning, adding more salt to taste.

Transfer the spread to a small serving plate or bowl. Drizzle with a generous amount of extra-virgin olive oil all over and sprinkle with *pul biber*. Serve with flatbreads or crackers.

✦ **Prepare ahead:** Fantastic to prepare ahead, it will keep in the refrigerator for 3–4 days if stored in an airtight container.

✦ **Serving suggestions:** Serve as part of a *meze* spread. We love it as a side to *Turkish Şakşuka* (page 108) with *Balon Ekmek* (page 44). It makes a fantastic spread in sandwiches, too.

Haydari

Strained Yoghurt Dip with Garlic and Herbs

Serves 4

This is a much-loved *meze*, enjoyed throughout the country. It is so easy to make yet packed with flavour; a wonderful, versatile accompaniment to savoury pastries, grills and casseroles. You will need to use strained (*süzme*, as we say in Turkish) yoghurt, to achieve the thick, creamy texture. I have seen variations of *haydari* where mashed feta or *beyaz peynir* is added, too – but I like to keep mine simple, as it is traditionally enjoyed. Dill, garlic and dried mint flavour it beautifully.

1 large garlic clove
sea salt, to taste
**450 g (1 lb) strained
  yoghurt**
**1 tablespoon finely
  chopped dill sprigs,**
  plus a few sprigs to garnish
1 teaspoon dried mint
**1 tablespoon extra-virgin
  olive oil**

Peel the garlic clove by crushing it with the flat side of a knife and the heel of your hand. Finely chop and sprinkle over a pinch of salt. Using the flat side of the knife, gently squash the chopped garlic to turn it into a fine paste.

In a medium bowl, combine the strained yoghurt with the garlic paste. Stir in the chopped dill and dried mint, and mix well. Check the seasoning, adding a little more salt if needed. Spoon onto a serving plate and drizzle with the extra-virgin olive oil. Garnish with a few dill sprigs and serve.

Mutabal

Smoked Aubergine with Tahini, Lemon Juice and Olive Oil

Serves 2-3

Mutabal, also known as *moutabal*, is a popular dip enjoyed all through the Levant, as well as in southern *Türkiye* (Turkey). It is another delicious way to enjoy smoked aubergine (eggplant), this time using silky tahini. You need to expose the aubergine to direct heat for that delicious, smoky flavour – you can barbecue it, too. It is fantastic as part of *meze* spread or as a side to grills, mains or savoury *böreks*. We traditionally enjoy *Mutabal* at room temperature.

2 medium aubergines (eggplant)
3 tablespoons freshly squeezed lemon juice
2 tablespoons tahini
1 large garlic clove, finely chopped
1 tablespoon extra-virgin olive oil, plus extra to serve
sea salt and freshly ground black pepper, to taste
1 tablespoon pomegranate seeds

Place the aubergines directly over the burner/stove top on a high heat and roast for about 25–30 minutes (depending on the size of the aubergines) until the skin is burnt and the flesh is soft, turning occasionally with metal tongs so that all sides cook evenly and the skin becomes nicely chargrilled.

Carefully place the blackened aubergines in a colander or sieve. When cool enough to handle, peel away the burnt skin and discard the stalks. With the flesh in the colander/sieve, gently squeeze to drain away any bitter juices.

Transfer to a chopping board and chop and mash the flesh, then transfer to a bowl. Add 2 tablespoons of the lemon juice so it doesn't discolour, and mix well. Stir in the tahini, garlic, extra-virgin olive oil and remaining lemon juice, then season with salt and pepper. Combine well.

Spoon the mixture onto a serving plate and spread. Sprinkle over the pomegranate seeds and drizzle with a little more extra-virgin olive oil, then serve.

+ **Prepare ahead:** *Mutabal* keeps well in the refrigerator for 2–3 days. You can prepare the smoked aubergine flesh a day ahead and keep covered in the refrigerator, too.

+ **Tip:** Place kitchen foil around the stove top/burner, taking care not to get it near to the flame, before placing the aubergine on top, for a less messy way of smoking the aubergine.

Cevizli, Yoğurtlu, Sarımsaklı Havuç ve Kabak

Garlicky Courgettes and Carrots with Walnuts in Yoghurt

Serves 4-6

This is a delightful, wholesome, versatile *meze*, also great with grills and pasta as well as a topping for a Turkish-style stuffed baked potato (*Kumpir*, page 166). The sweetness of sautéed garlicky carrots and courgettes (zucchini) works so well combined with the yoghurt and dill. I like adding chopped gherkins (or my *Salatalık Turşusu*, page 217) here for a touch of tanginess and crunchy walnuts for added texture and flavour.

3 medium courgettes
  (about 600 g/1 lb 5 oz),
  trimmed and grated
**sea salt and freshly ground
  black pepper,** to taste
**1 medium carrot (about
  200 g/7 oz),** trimmed and
  grated
4 tablespoons olive oil
4 garlic cloves, finely
  chopped
30 g (1 oz) gherkins,
  chopped (or Pickled
  Cucumbers, page 217)
**45 g (1¾ oz/⅓ cup) shelled
  walnuts,** chopped into
  bite-size pieces
handful of fresh dill, hard
  stalks removed, chopped
**280 g (10 oz/generous 1
  cup) full-fat yoghurt (or
  plant-based alternative)**
extra-virgin olive oil, to
  serve
sprinkle of *pul biber*, to
  serve

Place the grated courgette in a colander, sprinkle with a little salt and leave to drain for 10 minutes. Using a dish towel or sturdy paper towels, squeeze out any excess juice from the courgette and put in a large bowl. Add the grated carrots and combine.

Heat the olive oil in a wide heavy pan over a medium-high heat, add the grated mixture and sauté for 5 minutes, stirring often. Stir in the garlic, season with salt and pepper, and sauté for a further 3 minutes. The vegetables will soften up but still have a crunch to them. Transfer to a large bowl to cool.

Once cool, stir in the chopped gherkins, walnuts and dill, then fold in the yoghurt and combine well. Season again, if needed, and mix. Spread over a serving plate, drizzle over the extra-virgin olive oil, sprinkle over the *pul biber* and serve cold or at room temperature.

✦ **Prepare ahead:** You can prepare this *meze* a day ahead, cover and store in the refrigerator. Leftovers keep well for up to two days.

Zeytinli Mantar Sote

Sautéed Garlicky Mushrooms with Peppers and Olives

Serves 4

You would be served garlicky *mantar sote* at restaurants in *Türkiye* (Turkey) and this version with peppers and olives reminds me of our family holidays in the Aegean and Mediterranean regions, where some of the best olives are produced. Meaty mushrooms, sweet peppers and salty olives work well together in this juicy, refreshing *meze*.

6 tablespoons olive oil

280 g (10 oz) chestnut (cremini) mushrooms, cleaned with damp paper towels, halved and sliced

sea salt and freshly ground black pepper, to taste

1 medium red (bell) pepper, deseeded, cut into 8 wedges lengthways and thinly sliced widthways

4 garlic cloves, finely chopped

80 g (3 oz) good-quality green olives, sliced (I love olives – use less if preferred)

1 tablespoon fresh lemon juice

small handful of flat-leaf parsley, finely chopped

sprinkle of *pul biber*, to serve (optional)

Heat 4 tablespoons of the olive oil in a large, wide pan over a medium–high heat, add the mushrooms, season with salt and pepper, and sauté for 5 minutes, stirring continuously. They will soften and start to brown a little. Using a slotted spoon, transfer the cooked mushrooms to a plate.

Add the remaining 2 tablespoons of oil to the pan and stir in the sliced peppers. Sauté for 4 minutes, stirring often, then add the garlic, olives and sautéed mushrooms, and season with black pepper (be mindful of adding extra salt as olives are already salty). Combine well and cook for a further 3 minutes. Add the lemon juice and parsley, mix well and remove from the heat. Sprinkle *pul biber* over, if you like, and serve with crusty bread or flatbreads on the side.

✦ **Prepare ahead:** You can make *Zeytinli Mantar Sote* a day ahead and keep in the refrigerator, covered.

✦ **Serving suggestions:** As well as hot or cold *meze*, you can also serve *Zeytinli Mantar Sote* warm with pasta, rice, or with Turkish-style baked potatoes (*Kumpir*, page 166). My *Balon Ekmek* (page 44) would be lovely to mop up the delicious juices, too.

Meze

Fellah Köftesi

Bulgur Kofte with Tomato and Leafy Greens Sauce

Serves 4

This juicy, moist bulgur kofte is a winner with our vegetarian guests, not only as a *meze* but also as a main dish – they are delicious and substantial. There are many variations of bulgur kofte, and this *Fellah Köftesi* is especially popular in the Adana and Mersin regions in the south. Semolina is a key ingredient here, as it helps bind the bulgur kofte. You need to use fine bulgur for this recipe, nowadays widely available at online Turkish and Middle Eastern stores. My grandmother from Antakya would add *pazı* (chard) to the sauce – I love the slightly bitter greens with these koftes. You can substitute with spring greens or kale.

FOR THE BULGUR KOFTE
170 g (6 oz/1 cup) fine bulgur
160 ml (5½ oz/scant ¾ cup) hot water, plus 60 ml (2 fl oz/¼ cup)
70 g (2½ oz/generous ½ cup) semolina
1 tablespoon plain (all -purpose) flour, plus 1 tablespoon for shaping
2 tablespoons double concentrated tomato paste
1 tablespoon Turkish red pepper paste (*biber salçası*, see page 218 for homemade)
2 teaspoons ground cumin
sea salt and freshly ground black pepper, to taste
1 tablespoon olive oil, plus a drizzle for shaping

FOR THE SAUCE
200 g (7 oz) Swiss chard, spring greens or kale, hard stalk removed, thinly sliced
3 tablespoons olive oil
1 medium onion, chopped
3 garlic cloves, finely chopped
2 tablespoons double concentrated tomato paste
1 tablespoon Turkish red pepper paste (*biber salçası*, see page 218 for homemade)
1 tablespoon lemon juice
60 ml (2 fl oz/¼ cup) water
pul biber, to serve

First prepare the kofte. Rinse the bulgur in a sieve and press gently to get rid of excess moisture, then place in a large mixing bowl. Pour 160 ml (5½ oz/scant ½ cup) hot water over the bulgur, stir and leave to absorb for 7–8 minutes.

Stir the semolina, plain flour, tomato paste, pepper paste and ground cumin into the bulgur, and season with salt and pepper. Slowly pour in 60 ml (2 fl oz/½ cup) hot water and knead the mixture with your hands for 3–4 minutes until it resembles a soft, smooth dough. Check the seasoning, adding more salt or pepper to your taste.

Have a small bowl of room-temperature water with a drizzle of olive oil to help shape the kofte near you. Also prepare a wide tray scattered with 1 tablespoon of plain flour. Dampen your fingers in the bowl, take a large cherry-size piece of bulgur dough and shape into a ball. Gently press to make a dent in the middle of the kofte with your little finger, to make the traditional *Fellah Köftesi* shape (or leave as round kofte, if you prefer). Place the kofte on the tray and gently shake the tray so that all the kofte are coated with the flour.

Bring a large pan of salted water to the boil and gently drop in the kofte. Cook, uncovered, over a medium heat, for 8–10 minutes. Once cooked, the kofte will rise to the top of the pan. Remove with a slotted spoon and place in a large bowl. When all are cooked, drizzle with the tablespoon of olive oil and gently shake the bowl so that they are all coated and won't stick to one another. Set aside.

FOR THE SAUCE, pour plenty of hot water into a medium–large pan and add a pinch of salt. Add the chard or greens and cook for 3 minutes over a medium heat until softened. Drain and refresh under cold running water and set aside.

Heat the olive oil in a wide pan over a medium heat, add the onion and sauté for 8 minutes. Add the garlic, tomato and red pepper pastes, and stir for a minute, then add the prepared greens, lemon juice and 60 ml of water to the pan, season with salt and pepper and mix well. Add the kofte to the sauce and gently combine, then cook over a medium–low heat for 3–4 minutes.

Serve immediately, with a sprinkle of *pul biber* if you like.

+ **Prepare ahead:** This recipe is great for entertaining, as you can prepare both the bulgur kofte and the sauce ahead of time. It keeps well in the refrigerator for 2–3 days, covered.

Turkish Şakşuka

Baked Aubergines, Courgettes, Peppers with Tomato Sauce

Serves 2-3

You might know *Shakshuka* (meaning 'all mixed up') as a popular dish in the Middle East of eggs cooked in tomato sauce, peppers, herbs and sometimes onions. For us Turks, though, the name and dish *Şakşuka* refers to this delicious, summery *meze* of aubergines (eggplant) and peppers cooked in olive oil, served with a tomato-based sauce. Vegetables are traditionally shallow-fried in olive oil for this recipe, although for a lighter and equally tasty option, I prefer to bake them in the oven. I added courgettes (zucchini) here, too, following my mother's recipe.

1 large aubergine (eggplant), partially peeled in stripes and trimmed
sea salt and freshly ground black pepper, to taste
1 medium courgette (zucchini), cut into 1 cm (½ in) slices
1 red (bell) pepper, deseeded and cut into 3 cm (1 in) chunks
2-3 chillies or Turkish *sivri biber*, deseeded and sliced in half lengthways
4 tablespoons olive oil
flatbreads, to serve

FOR THE TOMATO SAUCE
1 tablespoon olive oil
3 garlic cloves, crushed with salt and finely chopped
400 g (14 oz) tin chopped tomatoes
2 teaspoons Turkish red pepper paste (*biber salçası*, see page 218 for homemade)
½ teaspoon *pul biber* or red pepper flakes (optional)
small handful of flat-leaf parsley, finely chopped
sea salt and freshly ground black pepper, to taste

FOR THE YOGHURT SAUCE
200 g (7 oz/generous ¾ cup) thick and creamy plain yoghurt (or plant-based alternative)
2 garlic cloves, finely chopped
sea salt and freshly ground black pepper, *to taste*

Preheat the oven to 200°C fan/220°C/425°F/gas 7.

Cut the peeled aubergine in half lengthways, then cut each half into 1 cm (½ in) slices. Place them on a large tray, sprinkle with salt and set aside for 10 minutes. Salt will help the moisture come out of the aubergines. Dry thoroughly with paper towels.

On a large baking tray, arrange the aubergine slices with the sliced courgette, pepper and chillies on the tray in one layer. Coat with olive oil and season with salt and pepper. Rub the seasoning and oil into the vegetables with your hands. Bake in the oven for 20 minutes. Remove the tray from the oven, remove the pepper strips and place on a large serving plate. Turn the aubergine and courgette slices and bake for a further 10 minutes until charred at edges and cooked through. Place alongside the peppers on the serving plate.

While the vegetables are baking, make the tomato sauce. Heat the olive oil in a wide pan over a medium heat, add the garlic and sauté for a minute, then add the chopped tomatoes and the pepper paste and mix well. Cook for 3-4 minutes until the sauce thickens. Stir in the *pul biber* (if using) and the parsley. Season with salt and pepper to taste and remove from the heat.

FOR THE YOGHURT SAUCE, beat the yoghurt with the garlic and season to taste with salt and pepper.

Spoon the tomato sauce over the top of the cooked vegetables. Serve with the yoghurt sauce on the side, accompanied by flatbreads to mop up the tasty sauce.

+ **Prepare ahead:** You can prepare *Şakşuka* a day ahead and keep covered in the refrigerator.

+ **Serving suggestion:** My mum would always serve this with the nutty *Muhammara* (page 97) and *Kekikli, Pul Biberli Fırın Patates* (page 174); they complement *Şakşuka* like a dream.

Öcce

Spring Onion Fritters with Fresh Herbs

Serves 4

These delightful, herby fritters are a popular specialty, especially in the Gaziantep, Kilis and Hatay regions. Locals make them with lots of spring onions (scallions), herbs and fresh garlic, when in season. There are many variations throughout the country, where, for instance, grated courgettes (zucchini) can be added too, as in our popular *kabak mücveri*. In the south, locals use a special *öcce* pan with hollows, where the batter is poured over to be shallow fried.
A regular, non-stick wide pan will work just as well.

6 spring onions (scallions), trimmed and finely chopped
5 garlic cloves, finely chopped
30 g (1 oz) fresh mint leaves, finely chopped
130 g (4¼ oz) flat-leaf parsley, finely chopped (including stems)
1 teaspoon *pul biber* or red pepper flakes
1 teaspoon ground cumin
85 g (3 oz/⅔ cup) plain (all-purpose) flour (use gram/chickpea flour for a gluten-free option)
55 g (2 oz) *beyaz peynir* or feta, crumbled (optional)
3 medium eggs, beaten
sea salt and freshly ground black pepper, to taste
light olive oil or groundnut oil, for shallow frying

Place the spring onions, garlic, fresh mint, parsley, *pul biber* and cumin in a large bowl. Using your hands, combine the mixture well. Add the flour and cheese (if using) and stir in the beaten eggs, then season with salt and pepper, and combine well into a batter.

Heat enough oil to cover the base of a large non-stick frying pan (skillet) (about 25 cm/10 in in diameter) over a medium–high heat. Drop tablespoons of the batter mix into the hot oil, spoonful by spoonful, leaving space between each one. Shallow fry for about 2 minutes on each side until golden brown. Remove with a slotted spoon to drain on paper towels.

+ **Serving suggestions:** *Haydari* dip (page 98) complements these fritters well. Why not make a delicious wrap with *Öcce*, *Bostana Salatası* (page 127) and *Muhammara* (page 97) over my *Balon Ekmek* (page 44).

Salata

Five

Salads

Salata

When I visit home, one of my favourite things to do is to go to the *pazar* (farmers' market). Our local *pazar* in 4th Levent, Istanbul, is a feast for the senses, with a breathtaking variety of vegetables, fruits, olives, nuts and cheeses galore on display – so inspiring. The huge variety of our Turkish salads showcase the bounty of *pazar*. There is simplicity in our salads, too; we mostly use olive oil and lemon juice for dressing, Mediterranean-style, and sometimes tahini, vinegar or pomegranate molasses can be added for regional salads. I am passionate about how healthy Turkish cuisine is and this chapter pays tribute to our nutritious salads, many of which are combined with wholegrains, nuts and legumes to make a wholesome and substantial dish.

Some of my personal favourites are *Tahinli Fasulye Piyazı* (Antalya-Style Bean Salad with Tahini Sauce, page 120), which is so moreish and easy to make; and *Patlıcanlı Ekşileme* (my Smoked Aubergine Salad, page 129), sunshine on a plate. Once you master how to smoke aubergine (eggplant), you will be able to enhance a huge variety of dishes, salads and dips with the deliciously smoky flesh. Try *Cevizli Bat Salatası* (page 123) for a substantial option – a specialty from the Black Sea region, combining earthy green lentils, fragrant *reyhan* (our basil) and crunchy walnuts, for delicious layers of flavour. Last but not least, I hope you have a go at *Karışık Mevsim Salatası* (page 124) – a firm family favourite, this refreshing, crunchy salad has been on our tables since I was a child.

Nohut Piyazı

Chickpea Salad with Sumac Onions

Serves 4-6

This is a delicious variation of the much-loved Turkish bean salad, *Fasulye Piyazı*. I love the earthy flavour of *nohut* (chickpeas/garbanzo beans) and they are fantastic paired with tangy sumac-infused onions in this refreshing, nutritious salad. As a matter of fact, citrussy sumac rubbed into the red onion slices is a key ingredient and makes this salad special for me – please do the rubbing with your hands, so that the sumac infuses well, for maximum flavour.

1 medium red onion, halved and thinly sliced
pinch of salt
1 teaspoon ground sumac (use more if you are a fan!), plus extra to serve
2 x 400 g (14 oz) tins pre-cooked chickpeas (garbanzo beans) (discard any loose skins)
2 medium, ripe tomatoes, finely chopped
1 red (bell) pepper, deseeded and finely chopped
3 spring onions (scallions), trimmed and finely chopped
small bunch of flat-leaf parsley, finely chopped

FOR THE DRESSING
3 tablespoons extra-virgin olive oil
juice of ½ lemon (about 2 tablespoons)
sea salt and freshly ground black pepper, to taste

Place the red onion slices in a large mixing bowl. Sprinkle with a pinch of salt and the ground sumac, then rub into the onion slices with your hands really well. This will soften the onions and make them more palatable, and will also help the tangy sumac infuse the onions.

Drain and rinse the chickpeas, then combine with the onions. Stir in the chopped tomatoes, peppers, spring onions and parsley, and combine well.

FOR THE DRESSING, mix the extra-virgin olive oil and lemon juice in a small container. Season with salt and pepper to taste.

Pour the dressing over the salad and combine well. Transfer to a serving plate and serve with an extra pinch of ground sumac sprinkled over.

+ **Tip:** If you prefer to use dried chickpeas, you need to soak them in cold water overnight. Drain and put them in a pan with plenty of fresh water, and cook for about 1 hour, or until tender, adding salt towards the end of the cooking time. Drain and set aside in a bowl, to be used in this salad.

+ **Serving suggestions:** Serve with flatbreads, *Balon Ekmek* (page 44), or *Mısır Ekmeği* (page 50) for a gluten-free option, on the side to mop up the delicious juices. *Salatalık Turşusu* (page 217) complement this salad, too.

Tahinli Fasulye Piyazı

Antalya-Style Bean Salad with Tahini Sauce

Serves 4

(GF) (VO)

We have a variety of bean salads and this *Tahinli Fasulye Piyazı* is a specialty from the Antalya region, on the southwest coast. It makes a substantial, nutritious, great-value lunch with flatbreads to mop up the delicious sauce.

2 x 400 g (14 oz) tins pre-cooked cannellini beans
½ small onion, quartered and thinly sliced
1 medium ripe tomato, diced
handful of flat-leaf parsley, finely chopped
45 g (1¾ oz/⅓ cup) Turkish or other good-quality black olives, pitted and halved
sea salt and freshly ground black pepper, to taste

FOR THE TAHINI SAUCE
2 fat garlic cloves, crushed and finely chopped
juice of ½ lemon
1 teaspoon ground cumin
pinch of salt
2 tablespoons tahini
1 tablespoon grape or cider vinegar
60 ml (2 fl oz/¼ cup) lukewarm water

TO SERVE
2 hard-boiled eggs, quartered (optional)
drizzle of extra-virgin olive oil

Drain and rinse the beans, then place in a large bowl. Stir in the onions and gently combine.

TO MAKE THE TAHINI SAUCE, combine the garlic, lemon juice, ground cumin and a good pinch of salt with the tahini in a small bowl. Stir and combine well; you will notice the sauce will thicken. Pour in the vinegar and lukewarm water, and combine well for 30 seconds. You will achieve a runny sauce at the end. Pour this sauce over the beans and gently combine well.

Stir the tomatoes, parsley and olives into the salad and combine well, then check the seasoning and adjust to your taste.

Transfer the salad to a serving plate, decorate with the quartered, hard-boiled eggs (if using), drizzle with extra-virgin olive oil and serve.

+ **Note:** If you prefer to use dried beans, you need to soak them in cold water overnight. Drain and put them in a pan with plenty of fresh water, and cook for about 1 hour, or until tender, adding salt towards the end of the cooking time. Drain and set aside in a bowl, to be used in this salad.

+ **Serving suggestions:** Enjoy with *Balon Ekmek* (page 44) or as a side to grills (broils). It is also lovely served with *Fırında Sebzeli Karnabahar Mücveri* (page 140).

Salata

Salata

Cevizli Bat Salatası

Green Lentil Salad with Walnuts

Serves 4–6

I first came across *Cevizli Bat* while following dear Sahrap Soysal's culinary travels to Tokat, in the Black Sea. Sahrap Hanım is one of my favourite food writers at home and I always admire her passion to bring out regional, wholesome Turkish flavours. This substantial salad has generous dressing and is traditionally served with Tokat's *ekşi mayalı ekmek* (sourdough bread) to dip in (the word bat derives from the verb *batırmak*, meaning 'to dip'), as well as with the region's vine leaves to use as a scoop. In the summer months, ice cubes can be added, too, which makes it a chilled, chunky soup consistency.

140 g (5 oz/¾ cup) green
  lentils, rinsed
700 ml hot water
sea salt and freshly ground
  black pepper, to taste
2 tablespoons double
  concentrated tomato
  paste
1 medium onion, finely
  chopped
4 spring onions (scallions),
  trimmed and finely
  chopped
3 medium, ripe tomatoes,
  finely chopped
1 tablespoon finely
  chopped fresh dill
2 tablespoons finely
  chopped flat-leaf parsley
2 teaspoons finely
  chopped fresh basil leaves
80 g (3 oz/⅔ cup) shelled
  walnuts, roughly chopped
1 teaspoon *pul biber*
vine leaves (fresh or in
  brine) or *ekşi mayalı
  ekmek* (sourdough bread),
  to serve

FOR THE DRESSING
3 tablespoons fresh
  lemon juice
170 ml (6 fl oz) water

Place the lentils in a medium pan with the measured hot water and a pinch of salt. Partially cover and bring to the boil, then simmer over a low heat for 25–30 minutes until the lentils are cooked but not mushy. Drain and rinse under running cold water, place in a large mixing bowl and let it cool.

Stir the tomato paste and chopped onions into the cooled lentils and combine well. Add the remaining vegetables, herbs and walnuts to the bowl.

FOR THE DRESSING, combine the lemon juice with the water in a small container. Pour over the salad, season with salt, pepper and *pul biber*, and gently combine.

Serve in shallow plates or bowls, with slices of *ekşi mayalı ekmek* (sourdough bread) on the side. It is lovely scooped and wrapped into fresh vine leaves, as the locals do. If using vine leaves in brine, rinse them well under running cold water a few times.

Karışık Mevsim Salatası

Zingy Salad with Red Cabbage, Carrot and Sweetcorn

Serves 4-6

Karışık Mevsim Salatası is a popular salad and we have it on our table often. My dear belated father Orhan was a lawyer with Karayolları, the Turkish Government's Transportation Department, and they have an employee *lokanta* (restaurant) in Ortaköy, Istanbul, where we used to go for family meals. This salad was one of the first things we would order when we went there.

150 g (5 oz) carrot, trimmed and grated

2 spring onions (scallions), trimmed and finely chopped

kernels of 1 medium corn cob, pre-cooked

60 g (2 oz) lettuce, coarsely chopped

juice of ½ lemon

1 tablespoon extra-virgin olive oil

sea salt and freshly ground black pepper, to taste

FOR THE QUICK-PICKLED RED CABBAGE

250 g (9 oz) red cabbage, quartered and finely sliced

2 tablespoons grape vinegar (or vinegar of your choice)

1 tablespoon extra-virgin olive oil

salt

Start with the quick-pickled red cabbage. Combine the sliced red cabbage with the vinegar and extra-virgin olive oil, and season with salt. With clean hands, rub the dressing into the cabbage, massaging and combining well. Cover and set aside for 10 minutes (longer if you can).

In a large bowl, combine all the salad vegetables with the quick-pickled red cabbage. Pour over the lemon juice and extra-virgin olive oil, season with salt and pepper, and mix well, ready to serve.

✦ **Serving suggestions:** I love *Karışık Mevsim Salatası* as part of *meze* and with pilafs such as *Nohutlu Pilav* (page 173). It also goes particularly well with my *Sebzeli, Mercimekli Lazanya* (page 203).

Bostana Salatası

Orchard Salad with Pomegranate Molasses

Serves 4-6

This is a juicy, refreshing salad from the Urfa region in the southeast. Vegetables are cut very finely in this salad and purslane or cucumber can be added, too. I love the refreshing fresh mint and parsley and the tanginess from the lemon and pomegranate molasses – the juice of unripe, sour grapes or plum can also be used instead in the dressing when in season. Locals may also add ice cubes to the salad, turning it into cold soup to eat with a spoon when it's very hot. Olive oil is not used in *Bostana* traditionally, but you can drizzle a little over before serving, if you wish.

½ **medium onion,** finely chopped

sea salt and freshly ground black pepper, to taste

1 **medium green (bell) pepper or 2 pointed peppers** (*sivri biber*), deseeded and finely chopped

3 **spring onions (scallions),** trimmed and finely chopped

3 **medium, ripe tomatoes,** finely chopped

small bunch of flat-leaf parsley, finely chopped

1 **tablespoon finely chopped fresh mint leaves**

1 **tablespoon pomegranate molasses** (*nar ekşisi*, see page 220 for homemade)

1 **tablespoon fresh lemon juice**

60 g (2 oz/¼ cup) **pomegranate seeds**

Place the chopped onions in a large bowl and sprinkle a little salt over. Rub the salt into the onions with your hands for a minute to soften. Stir in the peppers, spring onions, tomatoes, parsley and mint, and combine well.

In a small bowl, mix the pomegranate molasses with the lemon juice. Pour over the salad, season with salt and pepper, and combine well. Sprinkle the pomegranate seeds over, gently combine and serve.

+ **Serving suggestions:** This refreshing salad is a fantastic side to casseroles, *böreks*, or as *meze*. I also love it over toasted bread or flatbreads, combined with *Muhammara* (page 97).

Fırında Nar Ekşili, Peynirli İncir

Baked Figs with Feta in Pomegranate Molasses Sauce

Serves 4-6

We are a nation of fig lovers. My grandmother had fig (*incir*), pomegranate and walnut trees in her courtyard at our 450-year-old family home in Antakya, and it was always such a joy to pick ripe, juicy figs from the tree. Living abroad, I can't always get ripe, juicy figs so I find baking them in a marinade of honey, pomegranate molasses (*nar ekşisi*) and olive oil ramps up their flavour and brings sweet, slightly sour lushness. I bake them here with feta (use *beyaz peynir* if you can get it) – its melting creaminess is lovely with baked figs. Crushed nuts add a lovely crunch; I used chopped hazelnuts, although any nuts of your choice would work.

200 g (7 oz) Turkish *beyaz peynir* or creamy feta, drained
1 tablespoon olive oil
260 g (9½ oz) fresh, ripe figs
45 g (1¾ oz/⅓ cup) chopped hazelnuts (or your choice of nuts)
80 g (3 oz) rocket (arugula)
2 tablespoons pomegranate seeds
crackers or flatbreads, to serve

FOR THE POMEGRANATE MOLASSES SAUCE
2 tablespoons olive oil
1 tablespoon pomegranate molasses (*nar ekşisi*, see page 220 for homemade)
2 teaspoons runny honey

Preheat the oven to 200°C fan/220°C/425°F/gas 7. Line a 25 cm (10 in) baking dish with baking paper.

Pat the *beyaz peynir* or feta dry with sturdy paper towels. Coat the cheese with the olive oil and rub well with your hands, then place in the middle of the baking dish.

Slice the figs in half lengthways and place in a large bowl.

FOR THE POMEGRANATE MOLASSES SAUCE, combine the olive oil, pomegranate molasses and runny honey in a small bowl and mix thoroughly to dissolve. Pour the sauce over the figs and with clean hands rub the slices to coat them well. Place them around the cheese, spooning the remaining sauce over the figs.

Bake for 25–30 minutes until the feta and figs are softened and start to char around the edges.

Meanwhile, toast the chopped hazelnuts in a small pan over a medium heat for about 2 minutes until lightly browned. Turn the heat off and set aside to cool.

Arrange the rocket leaves over a large serving plate and scatter over the toasted hazelnuts. As soon as the feta and figs are baked, place the hot feta in the middle of the plate and scatter the figs around. Drizzle the remaining sauce in the baking dish over them. Sprinkle with pomegranate seeds and serve immediately, with crackers or flatbreads on the side.

Patlıcanlı Ekşileme

Smoked Aubergine Salad

Serves 4

This is a wonderful, refreshing salad from my hometown Antakya and one of my favourites, featuring our beloved aubergine (eggplant), *patlıcan*. Traditionally, the aubergine is cooked over an open fire or over direct heat on a burner – this really is the best way to achieve the smoky flavour. Refreshing *Patlıcanlı Ekşileme* is packed with flavour; a welcome *meze* for warm summer days. Don't skip the dried mint – it elevates the salad and adds an even more refreshing touch.

2 medium aubergines (eggplant)

3 tablespoons lemon juice

½ onion, finely chopped

sea salt and freshly ground black pepper

1 large tomato, finely chopped

1 green pointed (*sivri*) or small bell pepper, finely chopped

handful of fresh flat-leaf parsley, finely chopped

2 tablespoons extra-virgin olive oil

1 teaspoon dried mint

Place the aubergines directly over the burner/stove top on a high heat and roast for about 25-30 minutes (depending on the size of the aubergines), turning occasionally with metal tongs so that all sides cook evenly and the skin is nicely chargrilled. Cook until the skin is burnt and the flesh is soft.

Carefully place the blackened aubergines in a colander/sieve. When cool enough to handle, peel away the burnt skin and discard the stalks. Put the flesh in a colander and gently squeeze to drain away any bitter juices. Place the flesh on a chopping board and chop and mash.

Transfer the flesh to a bowl, pour 2 tablespoons of the lemon juice over to help retain its colour, and mix well.

In a separate dish, rub the onion with a pinch of salt with your hands. This softens the onion slightly, making it more palatable. Add the onion to the aubergine, along with the chopped tomatoes, peppers and parsley. Stir in the remaining lemon juice, extra-virgin olive oil and dried mint, then season with salt and pepper to taste. Gently mix well and serve.

+ **Tip:** Place kitchen foil around the stove top/burner, taking care not to get it near to the flame, before placing the aubergine on top, for a less messy way of smoking the aubergine.

+ **Serving suggestions:** I love this refreshing salad as part of a *meze* spread; it is fantastic with *böreks* such as *Patatesli Sodalı Börek* (page 43).

Kısır

Spicy Bulgur Wheat Salad with Pomegranate Molasses

Serves 6-8

I grew up eating wholesome *Kısır* almost daily at my grandmother's 450-year-old stone home in Antakya. She would make her own pomegranate molasses (*nar ekşisi*) using the pomegranates in her garden. The local name for *Kısır* is actually *sarma içi* in Antakya, meaning 'stuffing for vine leaves', as we would wrap *Kısır* in young vine leaves to eat. It is more than a bulgur salad for us; it is our memories, our heritage.

350 g (12 oz/2 cups) fine
  bulgur
1 teaspoon *pul biber* or red
  pepper flakes
2 tablespoons double
  concentrated tomato
  paste
1 tablespoon Turkish
  red pepper paste (*biber
  salçası*, see page 218 for
  homemade)
1 medium onion, finely
  chopped
sea salt and freshly ground
  black pepper, to taste
320 ml (11 fl oz/scant 1⅓
  cups) hot water
juice of 1 medium lemon
2 tablespoons pomegranate
  molasses (*nar ekşisi*, see
  page 220 for homemade)
60 ml (2 fl oz/¼ cup) extra-
  virgin olive oil
4 spring onions (scallions),
  trimmed and finely
  chopped
3 medium, ripe tomatoes,
  finely chopped
small bunch of flat-leaf
  parsley, finely chopped
110 g (3¾ oz/½ cup)
  pomegranate seeds
lettuce leaves or young
  vine leaves, to serve

Place the fine bulgur, *pul biber*, tomato paste, pepper paste and the chopped onion in a large bowl, season with salt and pepper, and knead thoroughly with clean hands for a minute – this will help all the flavours marry and the onion to soften. Pour the hot water over this mixture and stir, then leave to stand for about 10 minutes, stirring occasionally. The bulgur mixture should absorb all the water by the end of this period and will be of a dry consistency.

Add the lemon juice and pomegranate molasses along with the extra-virgin olive oil and knead well again. Stir in the spring onions, tomatoes and parsley, and combine well. Check the seasoning, add more salt if needed, and mix again.

Serve the *Kısır* in a bowl, garnished with the pomegranate seeds, with lettuce or young vine leaves on the side for scooping and wrapping.

+ Note: There are two main varieties of bulgur wheat available: fine and coarse bulgur. Fine bulgur is commonly used in salads whereas the coarse bulgur is used in pilafs and for stuffing vegetables. If you can't get fine bulgur, you can make this salad with coarse bulgur. In that case, use 270 ml (9½ fl oz/generous 1 cup) hot water for 170 g (6 oz/1 cup) coarse bulgur and cook over a low heat for 10-12 minutes, covered. Combine with the rest of the ingredients as directed in the recipe.

+ Variations: For a gluten-free version, replace the bulgur with quinoa, place it in a sieve and rinse under running cold water. Cook in a medium pan with plenty of hot water and a pinch of salt for 10-15 minutes until fully cooked. Drain and combine the cooked quinoa with the other ingredients.

+ Serving suggestions: *Kısır* is versatile and substantial. Serve with grills (broils), as a topping for *Kumpir* (page 166), or with savoury pastries, such as *Ispanaklı Gül Böreği* (page 38).

Zeytinyağlı

Six

Vegetables Cooked in Olive Oil

Zeytinyağlı

When it comes to cooking vegetables, we Turks are purists. We favour simplicity, letting the flavours of the vegetables speak for themselves with no-fuss techniques. One such approach is the wholesome *zeytinyağlı* – vegetables cooked in olive oil and a little water, flavoured with lemon juice, herbs and spices, as in our iconic *Imam Bayıldı* (page 154). Other popular methods are *sarma* and *dolma* – rolled and stuffed vegetables. When I was growing up, making *dolma* and *sarma* with my grandmother was always a special ritual. To make *Lahana Sarması* (page 146) we would gather under the pomegranate trees, each person allotted a task: someone would prepare the leaves; someone would make the filling; amid a constant flow of tea, coffee and conversation. The dish is a great example of the no-waste Turkish kitchen, as we would make *Kapuska* (page 146) with the trimmings.

There are regional specialties in this chapter, such as *Adesiye* (page 143) from my hometown Antakya, where vegetables and legumes are slowly cooked in olive oil and flavoured with pomegranate molasses and spices – so delicious. The recipes in this chapter can be prepared ahead and will taste even better the next day, once the flavours have had a chance to develop – a characteristic of *zeytinyağlıs*. Although traditionally eaten at room temperature or cold, you may enjoy them warm, too, like we do for the easy and delicious *Zeytinyağlı Pazı* (page 156) on cold days. I hope you enjoy the many wonderful possibilities that are available when cooking vegetables the Turkish way.

Zeytinli Patates Bastısı

Baked Potatoes with Onions, Tomatoes and Olives

Serves 4-6

This delightful potato bake makes use of the *bastı* method, a layered cooking technique dating back to the Ottoman period. Meat and vegetables are traditionally first sautéed then layered and gently pressed into a round dish. Turkish food writer Sahrap Soysal notes that this technique is also referred to as *oturtma*. This humble, great-value dish is very moreish, perfect for buffets as well as easy weekday meals. Leftovers are delicious enjoyed cold the next day, too.

4 tablespoons olive oil, plus extra as needed

3 medium or 2 large onions, quartered and thinly sliced

4 garlic cloves, finely chopped

650 g (1 lb 7 oz) roasting potatoes, cut into 3 cm (1 in) discs, 1 cm (½ in) thick

1 teaspoon dried oregano

½ teaspoon *pul biber*

sea salt and freshly ground black pepper, to taste

60 g (2 oz/⅓ cup) good-quality black olives (Turkish or kalamata), pitted and halved

3 medium, ripe tomatoes, halved, then sliced 5 mm (¼ in) thick

handful of flat-leaf parsley, finely chopped, to serve

Heat 2 tablespoons of the olive oil in a large, wide pan over a medium heat, add the onions and sauté for 10 minutes until softened and starting to caramelise. Add the garlic and sauté for 2 minutes. Transfer to a plate and set aside.

Preheat the oven to 180°C fan/200°C/400°F/gas 6.

Add the remaining 2 tablespoons of oil to the same pan, add the potatoes and sauté over a medium heat for 5–6 minutes. Stir the onions back into the pan, season with salt, pepper, oregano and *pul biber*, combine well and remove from the heat.

Spread half of the potato and onions in the base of a 25 cm (10 in) baking dish. Layer over half of the olives and sliced tomatoes and gently press. Top with the remaining potato and onions, finishing with a final layer of olives and tomatoes, and gently press again. Drizzle with a little olive oil, season with salt and pepper, and bake for 40–45 minutes until fully cooked and charred at the edges.

Scatter with the chopped parsley and serve warm or at room temperature.

+ **Serving suggestion:** Enjoy *Zeytinli Patates Bastısı* with refreshing *Karışık Mevsim Salatası* (page 124).

Zeytinyağlı

Fırında Sebzeli Karnabahar Mücveri

Baked Cauliflower, Peppers, Carrots, Herbs and Feta

Serves 6–8

Mücver is a much-loved Turkish-style fritter, especially popular made with grated courgette (zucchini). Growing up in *Türkiye* (Turkey), my mother would make an easier, lighter and equally delicious baked version of *mücver*, using whatever vegetables she had to hand. Inspired by this, I have revisited a recipe from my debut book, *Özlem's Turkish Table*, and included carrots and peppers to create this *Sebzeli Karnabahar Mücveri*. It is a lovely bake that can accommodate other veg that needs using up – try thinly sliced courgettes or grated beets as variations. I also added some ground sumac, as its tangy flavour is lovely combined with the sweetness from the vegetables. Please use the cauliflower's outer leaves – they are too good to waste.

1 medium cauliflower
1 onion, finely chopped
1 red (bell) pepper, deseeded and sliced into 1 cm (½ in) chunks
1 red chilli pepper, deseeded and finely chopped
1 small carrot, grated
4 spring onions (scallions), finely chopped
small bunch of fresh dill, hard stems removed, finely chopped
small bunch of flat-leaf parsley, finely chopped
200 g (7 oz) Turkish white cheese, *beyaz peynir* or feta, drained and crumbled
60 ml (2 fl oz/¼ cup) olive oil, plus 1 tablespoon for greasing
2 teaspoons ground sumac
sea salt and freshly ground black pepper, to taste
4 medium eggs, beaten
85 g (3 oz/⅔ cup) plain (all-purpose) flour

Preheat the oven to 180°C fan/200°C/400°F/gas 6.

Cut the cauliflower into very small florets, rinse and drain. Discard the hard stalk, rinse the outer leaves, then slice into 1 cm (½ in) pieces. Place in a large bowl. Add the onion, pepper, chilli, carrot, spring onions, dill and parsley, then stir in the crumbled cheese, olive oil and sumac, and season with salt and pepper. With clean hands, combine the mixture well (at this stage, you can check the seasoning again and adjust to your taste). Stir in the beaten eggs and flour, and combine well.

Grease the base and sides of a 27 × 18 x 5 cm (11 × 7 × 2 in) baking dish with the tablespoon of oil. Tip the vegetable mixture into the baking dish and gently press down with your hands so everything is intact and evenly placed. Bake for 35–40 minutes until it has a nice light brown colour on top.

Slightly cool for 5 minutes, then slice and serve.

+ **Prepare ahead and tips:** You can use chickpea (gram) flour to make this gluten-free. You can bake ahead and reheat at 180°C fan/200°C/400°F/ gas 6 for 10 minutes before serving. It is also delicious served at room temperature.

+ **Serving suggestions:** Combine this delicious bake with cooling *Haydari* (page 98) and perhaps with *Salatalık Turşusu* (page 217).

Zeytinyağlı

Vegetables Cooked in Olive Oil

Adesiye

Pumpkin, Lentils and Chickpeas with Pomegranate Molasses

Serves 6–8

Adesiye is a delicious and wholesome specialty from my hometown Antakya. The colourful pumpkin and red peppers in this dish brighten grey days and it is wholesome with green lentils and chickpeas (garbanzo beans), too – the kind of food I love eating. This dish is a typical Antakya affair, where vegetables and legumes are slowly cooked together in olive oil and flavoured with pomegranate molasses and spices – scrumptious. Dried mint is important here as it really elevates the taste and adds a refreshing touch.

140 g (5 oz/¾ cup) green lentils
60 ml (2 fl oz/¼ cup) olive oil
2 medium onions, quartered and thinly sliced
3 medium red (bell) peppers, deseeded, quartered and thinly sliced
1.2 kg (2 lb 6 oz) pumpkin, peeled, deseeded and cut into 3 cm (1 in) chunks (prepared weight)
6 garlic cloves, finely chopped
400 g (14 oz) tin pre-cooked chickpeas (garbanzo beans), drained and rinsed (discard any loose chickpea skins)
2 tablespoons dried mint
1 teaspoon *pul biber*
sea salt and freshly ground black pepper, to taste

FOR THE SAUCE
45 g (1¾ oz/2 heaped tablespoons) double concentrated tomato paste
2 tablespoons pomegranate molasses (*nar ekşisi*, see page 220 for homemade)
650 ml (22 fl oz/generous 2½ cups) water
2 tablespoons olive oil

Put the lentils in a medium saucepan, pour in enough hot water to cover the lentils by 4 cm (1½ in), partially cover and simmer for 13 minutes. Drain and set the partially cooked lentils aside.

Heat the olive oil in a wide, heavy, deep sauté pan over a medium heat, add the onions and peppers and sauté for 8 minutes, stirring often. Add the pumpkin, lentils, garlic and chickpeas, season to taste and mix well.

Combine the sauce ingredients in a jug and pour into the pan, season with salt and pepper, and mix well. Cover and bring to the boil, then turn the heat down to a simmer for about 55 minutes, or until everything is cooked through (gently mix once halfway and do not mix further during cooking so that the pumpkin doesn't break up).

Remove from the heat, stir in the dried mint and *pul biber*, and gently combine. Cover and rest for 15 minutes before serving. *Adesiye* is a meal in itself served with crusty bread on the side to mop up the delicious juices.

✦ **Prepare ahead:** *Adesiye* tastes even better the next day and is a great dish to prepare ahead. This recipe makes a generous amount and keeps well in the refrigerator, covered, for 2–3 days.

Zeytinyağlı Biber Dolması

Stuffed Peppers with Aromatic Rice

Serves 4-6

This delicious *dolma* is my husband Angus's favourite. We had a long-distance courtship before getting married, as I was based in Istanbul and he was in Scotland. Every time he visited us at my parents' home in Istanbul, mum made sure that this was on the table. It is a special food for us with its rituals – family members gather and make *dolma* together; some prepare the vegetables; some the filling; a real social event that always brings happy childhood memories. There are many variations of *dolma* at home, but one thing consistent in *zeytinyağlı dolma* is the generous use of onions and olive oil, which add oodles of flavour.

12 Turkish green peppers or 7-8 green (bell) peppers
2 medium tomatoes, each sliced into 6 wedges
lemon wedges, to serve

FOR THE FILLING
4 tablespoons olive oil
3 medium onions, grated
3 tablespoons dried currants, soaked in warm water for 10 minutes and drained (optional)
3 tablespoons pine nuts
170 g (6 oz/¾ cup) short-grain rice, rinsed in warm water and drained
1 teaspoon sugar
1 teaspoon ground cinnamon
sea salt and freshly ground black pepper, to taste
300 ml (10 fl oz/1¼ cups) hot water
2 tablespoons finely chopped flat-leaf parsley
1 tablespoon finely chopped dill

FOR THE SAUCE
3 tablespoons olive oil
juice of ½ lemon
400 ml (13 fl oz/generous 1½ cups) hot water

Start with the filling. Heat the olive oil in a medium pan over a medium heat, add the onions and cook for 10 minutes, stirring often, until softened and lessened in volume. Stir in the currants (if using) and pine nuts, and combine well, then stir in the rice, sugar and cinnamon, season with salt and pepper, and give it all a good mix. Pour in the measured hot water and combine well, then cover and cook for 12 minutes over a low–medium heat until all the liquid is absorbed and the rice is partially cooked. Remove from the heat, stir in the chopped herbs and combine well. Check the seasoning and add more salt if needed. Set aside to cool for 10 minutes.

Meanwhile, prepare the peppers. Carefully slice the top of the peppers, saving the stalk ends. Using a small knife, carefully scoop out and discard the seeds and trim the inner white parts.

Take a couple of spoonfuls of the filling and gently pack into the peppers. Take care not to overfill – leave about 2 cm (¾ in) space at the top, as the rice will expand. Tightly pack the stuffed peppers upright in a wide, heavy pan (about 28 cm/11 in in diameter and 7 cm/3 in high), side by side. Place a wedge of tomato over the top of each pepper, then place the reserved stalk ends on top of each pepper.

Combine the sauce ingredients in a jug and carefully pour by the sides of the peppers (the liquid will come about a third of the way up the sides of the peppers). Cover the pan and cook over a low–medium heat for about 35 minutes until the *dolma* are cooked. Turn the heat off and let the *dolma* cool in the pan.

Serve at room temperature (or cold), with lemon wedges on the side.

+ Serving suggestion: Pair these delicious *dolma* with cooling *Haydari* (page 98) and *Otlu Tava Böreği* (page 40) for a complete meal.

Bulgurlu Lahana Sarması ve Kapuska

Cabbage Rolls with Bulgur, Pomegranate Molasses and Kapuska

Serves 4-6

Cabbage rolls are ubiquitous, with variations throughout Europe, especially in Eastern Europe, the Middle East, China and Russia (the word *kapusta* means 'cabbage' in several Slavic languages). This is how we enjoy cabbage rolls in the south, with nutty bulgur, sautéed onions and tangy pomegranate molasses.

This was one of my favourite comfort foods growing up and always stirs up good memories – that anticipation of *sarma* cooking and the irresistible 'quality control' bite from the pan to make sure it's cooked – happy days. It is another great example of Turkish frugality, as we use the chopped hard stalk and smaller leaves to go on and make *Kapuska*, with the addition of bulgur or rice (a sort of easier, deconstructed *sarma*). I cook them in the same pan so you get two dishes in one – both great value, wholesome and delicious. Large leaves are best to roll; if you can't get a large cabbage, use Savoy cabbage or a pointy sweetheart cabbage instead.

650 g (1 lb 7 oz) large white cabbage (or Savoy or sweetheart cabbage)

1 tablespoon olive oil

2 tablespoons lemon juice

1 tablespoon double concentrated tomato paste

sea salt and freshly ground black pepper, to taste

4 garlic cloves, coarsely chopped

plain yoghurt (or plant-based alternative), to serve

FOR THE FILLING

2 tablespoons olive oil

2 medium onions, finely chopped

3 garlic cloves, finely chopped

200 g (7 oz/scant 1¼ cups) coarse bulgur, rinsed

2 tablespoons flat-leaf parsley, finely chopped

1 teaspoon *pul biber*

2 teaspoons dried mint

1 tablespoon pomegranate molasses (*nar ekşisi*, see page 220 for homemade)

1 tablespoon double concentrated tomato paste

sea salt and freshly ground black pepper, to taste

FOR THE FILLING, heat the olive oil in a wide pan over a medium-high heat, add the onions and sauté for 10 minutes. Stir in the garlic and sauté for a further 2 minutes, then leave to cool for 5 minutes.

Combine the bulgur, parsley, *pul biber*, dried mint, pomegranate molasses and tomato paste in a large bowl and stir in the onions. Season with salt and pepper, and knead well with your hands to mix thoroughly. Check the seasoning and adjust to your taste.

Trim the bottom root of the cabbage and place it whole into a large pan. Pour over boiling water to cover and simmer for 6–7 minutes until the leaves are softened. Drain and refresh under cold running water. Use a sharp knife to cut the outer leaves from the main stalk. The rest of the leaves will start to peel off without breaking, one by one. Peel off about 16 large–medium leaves for rolling and set them aside. Carefully trim and make a V-shape cut to remove the thickest part of the stalk from the base of each cabbage leaf. Roughly chop these stalks, as well as the very small leaves not fit to roll, and place them on the base of a large saucepan or pot. Place the prepared cabbage leaves on a large plate for rolling later.

Combine the tablespoon of olive oil with the lemon juice (I do like it quite tangy, use less if you prefer) and tomato paste in a small bowl, and season with salt and pepper. Scatter the coarsely chopped garlic over the chopped cabbage stalks in the pot and pour the lemon mixture over. Combine well with a spoon and spread as the base layer for the cabbage rolls.

TO PREPARE THE ROLLS, place about 1 tablespoon of the filling (depending on the size of the leaf) in a line in the middle of a leaf. Fold in the sides and then roll the leaf up tightly. Repeat with the remaining leaves and filling. (Save any leftover filling for *Kapuska*.) Place the rolled leaves tightly in the pan, seam-sides down, layering and packing tightly.

FOR THE SAUCE
460 ml (16 fl oz/1¾ cups)
water
1 tablespoon olive oil
1 tablespoon pomegranate
molasses (*nar ekşisi,* see
page 220 for homemade)
sea salt and freshly ground
black pepper, to taste

FOR THE SAUCE, mix together the water, olive oil and pomegranate molasses in a jug, and season with salt and pepper. Pour this sauce over the cabbage rolls (it should just about cover the top of the rolls). Place a heatproof plate on top of the rolls to stop them unravelling during cooking. Cover the pan and cook over a low heat for 35–40 minutes, simmering gently.

Once the cabbage rolls are cooked, take out the plate with oven gloves, then place the cabbage rolls on a serving dish and cover until ready to serve.

TO MAKE KAPUSKA, stir the remaining filling (if not enough, add a little more bulgur to make 90 g (3 oz) mixture in total) into the pan with the cooked cabbage stalks and sauce. Season, combine well, then cover and cook over a low heat for 12–15 minutes until the bulgur is cooked and the liquid is absorbed.

Serve *Bulgurlu Lahana Sarması* and *Kapuska* warm with a dollop of yoghurt on the side. They are also delicious at room temperature.

Zeytinyağlı Kabak Çiçeği Dolması

Stuffed Courgette Flowers with Herby Rice and Pine Nuts

Serves 4-6

(V) (GF)

These stuffed courgette (zucchini) flowers, popular especially in the Aegean and Mediterranean regions, are summer on a plate for me. They always remind me of happy family holidays in Bodrum, as we would eat platefuls of these at the beachside cafés.

1 tablespoon pine nuts
30-35 courgette (zucchini) flowers (depending on their size)
2 tablespoons olive oil
1 small onion, very finely chopped
1 small tomato, grated
110 g (3¾ oz/generous ½ cup) long-grain rice, rinsed
2 teaspoons ground cinnamon
sea salt and freshly ground black pepper, to taste
110 ml (3¾ fl oz/scant ½ cup) hot water
2 tablespoons finely chopped fresh dill
2 tablespoons finely chopped flat-leaf parsley
lemon wedges, to serve

FOR THE SAUCE
2 tablespoons olive oil
2 tablespoons lemon juice
200 ml (7 fl oz/scant 1 cup) hot water

Toast the pine nuts in a hot, dry pan until golden, stirring often. Place on a small plate and set aside.

To prepare the courgette flowers, gently remove the stamen from inside (the flowers are delicate, so go slowly and handle with care). Cut the tip off the opposite end and the little outer leaves around the flower. Give a gentle rinse and place on a large plate.

Heat the olive oil in a medium pan over a medium–high heat, add the onion and sauté for 5 minutes until softened. Stir in the grated tomato (I finely chop the remaining bits and skin to add to the mixture), pine nuts and the rinsed rice, and combine well. Add the ground cinnamon, season with salt and pepper, and pour in the measured hot water. Stir, cover, bring to the boil, then reduce to a simmer for 8 minutes until the liquid is absorbed and the rice is partially cooked. Transfer to a large bowl to cool for 10 minutes.

Once cool, stir in the chopped dill and parsley. Check the seasoning, add more salt if needed, and combine well.

Gently open a flower and spoon in about 2 teaspoons of filling. Gently press the stuffing to remain intact and try not to overfill. Close the petals in a criss-cross pattern if you can, or swirl to seal, tucking the end of the petals under the flower. Place in a medium saucepan, with the top part facing the outer side of the pan. Stuff the remaining flowers in this way, placing them snugly side by side. They should cover the bottom of the pan.

Combine all the sauce ingredients and season with salt, then pour over the stuffed flowers. Place a heatproof flat plate over the stuffed flowers (so that they remain intact), cover with a lid and bring to the boil, then reduce to a low simmer for about 25 minutes until cooked through.

Remove from the heat, carefully take out the heatproof plate with oven gloves, then put the lid back on and let the *dolma* cool in the pan. Serve at room temperature or cold, with lemon wedges on the side.

+ **Prepare ahead:** These *dolma* will keep, covered, in the refrigerator for 2-3 days.

+ **Serving suggestions:** You can serve these delightful *dolma* as part of a *meze* spread. Include *Cevizli Bat Salatası* (page 123) and *Patatesli Sodalı Börek* (page 43) for a substantial meal.

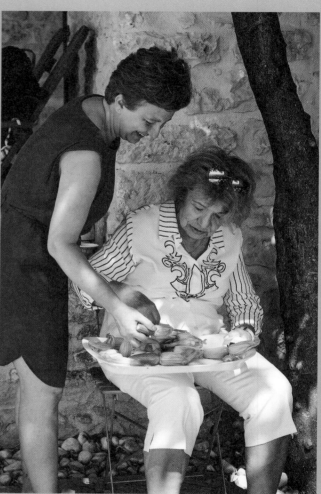

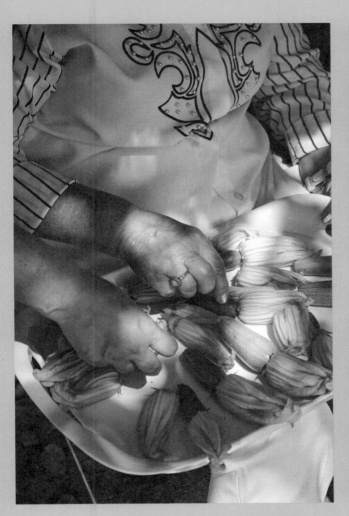

Zeytinyağlı Kereviz

Celeriac, Carrots and Peas Cooked in Olive Oil

Serves 4

Celeriac (celery root) is a knobbly root closely related to celery. It has a wonderful, earthy aniseed flavour and is packed full of goodness. Easy to make, healthy and delicious, *Zeytinyağlı Kereviz* is especially popular in the Aegean and Marmara regions, and is one of my husband's favourites. The lemon and olive oil sauce adds a lovely, refreshing taste; we traditionally add a little sugar to balance the flavours, too. I also like to add some peas; their natural sweetness complements celeriac well. If you have the celeriac leaves, please chop them and add to the dish. We also use the long, leafy celeriac stalks when making pickles, such as *Patlıcan Turşusu* (page 214), another fine example of the no-waste Turkish kitchen.

875 g (1 lb 15 oz) celeriac (celery root) (550 g/1 lb 3½ oz prepared weight), peeled, quartered and cut into 1 cm (½ in) chunks

juice of 2 lemons

80 ml (3 fl oz/generous ⅓ cup) olive oil

1 medium onion, quartered and thinly sliced

1 medium carrot, trimmed, halved lengthways and sliced into 1 cm (½ in) half moons

sea salt, to taste

225 ml (8 fl oz/scant 1 cup) water

½ teaspoon sugar

2 tablespoons peas, fresh or frozen

2 tablespoons finely chopped fresh dill

lemon wedges, to serve (optional)

Place the prepared celeriac in a bowl, squeeze over the juice of the first lemon and rub into the celeriac pieces – this will help prevent discolouration.

Heat the olive oil in a medium, heavy pan over a medium heat, add the onion and carrot, and sauté for 4–5 minutes. Stir in the celeriac, add the juice of the second lemon, the measured water, season with salt and add the sugar, and combine everything well. Bring to the boil, then reduce to a simmer, cover and cook for 25–30 minutes until the vegetables are almost cooked.

Add the peas and cook for a further 3–4 minutes. Check the seasoning and add more salt if needed. Turn the heat off, add the chopped dill (reserving a little for serving) and gently combine well. Cover and rest for at least 15 minutes.

Serve warm or at room temperature, with a little garnish of dill and lemon wedges on the side, if you like.

+ **Prepare ahead:** This lovely dish tastes even better the next day, as the flavours develop, and will keep well in the refrigerator, covered, for 2–3 days.

+ **Serving suggestions:** This lovely dish accompanies grills (broils) beautifully, or can be enjoyed as part of a *meze*. Why not also combine with *Otlu Tava Böreği* (page 40) for a delicious, substantial meal.

Vegetables Cooked in Olive Oil

İmam Bayıldı

Stuffed Aubergines Cooked in Olive Oil

Serves 4

İmam Bayıldı is probably one the most famous dishes at home, enjoyed since the Ottoman period, showcasing our beloved aubergine (eggplant), *patlıcan*. The aubergines are gently poached or baked in the oven, stuffed with a mixture of onions, peppers, tomatoes and garlic in generous olive oil, and served either cold or at room temperature. Absolutely delicious and refreshing for hot summer days, it just melts in the mouth.

2 medium aubergines (eggplant)
5 tablespoons olive oil
2 medium tomatoes
2 medium onions, quartered and thinly sliced
1 small green (bell) pepper or 2 small pointed green peppers (*sivri biber*), finely chopped
4 garlic cloves, finely chopped
sea salt and freshly ground black pepper, to taste
½ teaspoon sugar
handful of flat-leaf parsley, finely chopped

FOR THE SAUCE
juice of ½ small lemon
225 ml (8 fl oz/scant 1 cup) water
2 tablespoons olive oil

Preheat the oven to 200°C fan/220°C/425°F/gas 7.

Using a vegetable peeler, peel the aubergines lengthways in zebra stripes, then cut in half lengthways. In each half of the aubergine, cut a deep split lengthways without cutting through to the skin on the opposite side and leaving about 1 cm (½ in) uncut at either end. Place the halves on a tray, split sides facing up and sprinkle with salt (this will help the moisture come out). Set aside for 10 minutes. After that, thoroughly pat dry with sturdy paper towels, otherwise the aubergines will be soggy.

Place the prepared aubergines on a clean, large baking sheet, split sides facing up. Pour ½ tablespoon olive oil into each half and rub to coat well. Bake for 25 minutes until softened and the edges have started to brown. Remove and reduce the oven temperature to 180°C fan/200°C/400°F/gas 6.

While the aubergines are baking, prepare the filling. Grate the tomatoes and finely chop the remaining bits, including the skin, and place in a bowl.

Heat the remaining 3 tablespoons of olive oil in a large, wide pan over a medium–high heat, add the onions and sauté for 8 minutes, stirring often. Stir in the peppers and cook for 5 minutes, then add the tomatoes and garlic and cook for a further 2 minutes until the sauce has thickened. Season with salt and pepper, add the sugar and combine well. Remove from the heat and stir in the chopped parsley.

Place the aubergines side by side in a deep baking dish (about 25 × 18 cm/ 10 × 7 in) and gently open up the split in the middle to create pockets. Spoon the filling mixture into these pockets, packing some over the top, too.

Mix together the sauce ingredients and season with salt and pepper. Gently pour the sauce into the tray. Cover the dish with kitchen foil and bake for 25 minutes, then remove the foil, spoon the juices in the dish over the aubergines and bake for a further 20 minutes until the aubergines are tender and starting to caramelise on top.

Remove from the oven and put the foil back on to cover. Set aside to cool and let the flavours settle, then carefully transfer to a serving plate, spooning the juices from the dish over the aubergines. Serve at room temperature or cold.

✦ **Serving suggestion:** Combine with *Cevizli Bat Salatası* (page 123) for a wholesome meal.

Zeytinyağlı

Zeytinyağlı Pazı

Chard Cooked in Olive Oil with Onion, Peppers and Rice

Serves 4

This is a lovely and easy dish to enjoy *pazı* (chard), grown mostly in the northwest, Black Sea, Marmara, Aegean and Mediterranean regions. Its gently tart flavour is delicious here. These large leaves are also used for making *pazı sarması* (rolled chard leaves with aromatic rice and sometimes with fresh Turkish curd cheese, *lor peyniri*). On cold days, we enjoy it hot with a dollop of yoghurt and a drizzle of extra-virgin olive oil on top.

2 tablespoons olive oil

1 medium red or yellow onion, finely chopped

1 red chilli, deseeded and finely chopped (use more if you like it spicy)

4 garlic cloves, finely chopped

1 tablespoon double concentrated tomato paste

230 g (8 oz) tin chopped tomatoes

450g (1 lb) chard, cleaned, halved lengthways and roughly chopped into 1 cm (½ in) pieces

85 g (3 oz/scant ½ cup) long-grain rice, rinsed

460 ml (16 fl oz/scant 2 cups) hot water

sea salt and freshly ground black pepper, to taste

TO SERVE (OPTIONAL)

plain yoghurt (or plant-based alternative)

drizzle of extra-virgin olive oil

Heat the olive oil in a large, wide saucepan over a medium–high heat, add the onion and sauté for 3–4 minutes until starting to soften. Add the chilli, garlic, tomato paste and chopped tomatoes to the pan (save the tin for later), combine well and cook for 2 minutes. Stir in the chopped chard and gently combine and wilt over a medium heat for 2–3 minutes. Add the rinsed rice and combine well.

Rinse the chopped tomato tin with some of the hot water and pour all the liquid into the pan, season with salt and pepper, give it a good stir, then cover and cook for 20–25 minutes over a low–medium heat until the rice and vegetables are cooked. Turn the heat off and leave to rest for 10 minutes, covered.

When the weather is warm, we traditionally eat this dish cold or at room temperature. On cold days, we enjoy it hot with a dollop of yoghurt and a drizzle of extra-virgin olive oil over.

+ **Prepare ahead and variations:** This dish is great to prepare ahead – in fact, leftovers taste even better the next day as the flavours develop, a characteristic of *zeytinyağlı* dishes. You can use spinach or large leafy collard greens instead of chard. You can also use bulgur (not gluten-free) or quinoa (gluten-free) instead of rice.

+ **Serving suggestions:** Serve crusty bread or my gluten-free Corn Bread (page 50) on the side to mop up the delicious juices, if you like.

Sokak Yemekleri

Seven

Street Food

Sokak Yemekleri

W e have a vibrant street food scene in *Türkiye* (Turkey) – there is always a stall in sight, selling anything from sweet and savoury pastries to fresh orange and pomegranate juice, roasted chestnuts, corn, pickles and more. *Simit*, our iconic sesame-encrusted bread rings, are probably the most famous, available in almost every neighbourhood, with regional variations. You can enjoy *simit* for breakfast, or for a mid-morning or afternoon snack with *çay* (Turkish tea).

Kumpir (Turkish-style stuffed baked potatoes) has to be one of my favourite street foods. Growing up as a student in Istanbul, after school I would go with my friends down to Ortaköy district, famous for the *kumpir* street stalls. We would each fill our baked potato with the various fillings on offer – from sliced pickles to olives, sautéed mushrooms, cheese, and more – and enjoy it by the Bosphorus, overlooking the boats passing by. And how can one resist freshly baked *gözleme*, effortlessly made by locals in round *sac* ovens. Every time I visit our farmers' market (*pazar*) in Istanbul, it's a ritual to stop by the *gözleme* stall and enjoy with a glass of *çay*, watching the buzzing *pazar*. You will be pleasantly surprised how easy and satisfying it is to make *Patatesli, Ispanaklı Gözleme* at home (page 170).

This chapter pays tribute to some of my favourite Turkish street foods, including the ever delicious and easy *Nohut Dürümü* (spiced chickpea wrap, page 164), a Gaziantep specialty. My version omits the meat but I promise it's still packed full of flavour, combined with zingy *piyaz* salad in a wrap; great value, too.

I truly hope you enjoy recreating delights from our streets in your own kitchen and that they may bring happy memories back or inspire you to travel to my country and enjoy them in situ.

SOĞUK
SU
BULUNUR

ˈSiMiTÇiˈ

Nohut Dürümü

Spiced Chickpea Wrap with Piyaz Salad

Serves 2

Nohut Dürümü is a specialty in Gaziantep, especially in the Nizip region. Traditionally, dried chickpeas (garbanzo beans) are cooked with chunks of meat on the bone in a large pot. I omit the meat in my version and use a tin of good-quality pre-cooked chickpeas. In this easy wrap, sautéing and crushing the chickpeas over the warming cumin and *pul biber*-infused oil adds so much flavour. They are fantastic combined with the zingy *piyaz* salad with sumac onions and make a satisfying, great value meal.

60 ml (2 fl oz/¼ cup)
  olive oil
2 teaspoons ground
  cumin
1 teaspoon *pul biber* (use
  more if you like the heat)
1 x 400 g (14 oz) tin
  pre-cooked chickpeas
  (garbanzo beans), drained
  and rinsed (discard any
  loose skins)
sea salt, to taste
2 large or 4 small
  flatbreads, to serve

FOR THE PIYAZ SALAD
½ teaspoon ground sumac
sea salt and freshly ground
  black pepper, to taste
1 small red or yellow
  onion, halved and thinly
  sliced
1 small pointed red
  pepper or ½ large red
  (bell) pepper, deseeded
  and finely chopped
1 medium tomato, diced
handful of flat-leaf
  parsley, finely chopped
1 tablespoon extra-virgin
  olive oil
juice of ½ small lemon

First prepare the *piyaz* salad. In a bowl, thoroughly rub the sumac and a pinch of salt into the onion slices with your hands (this will soften the onions and help the sumac to infuse). Stir in the chopped pepper, tomato and parsley, and combine well. Whisk together the olive oil and lemon juice and pour over the salad. Season with more salt (if needed) and freshly ground black pepper. Set aside.

FOR THE CHICKPEAS, heat the olive oil in a wide, heavy pan over a medium heat, stir in the ground cumin and *pul biber* and combine well for 1–2 minutes to let the spices infuse the oil. Stir in the cooked chickpeas, season with salt and mix well so that they all have the spiced oil coating. With the back of the spoon, crush about half of the chickpeas (this helps the chickpeas to absorb the spiced oil, as well as bringing extra texture) and sauté for another 2–3 minutes. Check the seasoning and add more salt, if needed.

Place the flatbreads on serving plates. Spoon the spiced chickpeas in the middle of each flatbread, top with the *piyaz* salad and roll up.

+ **Note:** You can use dried chickpeas here; if so, you need to soak them in cold water overnight, drain, then put them in a pan with plenty of fresh water. Cook for about 1 hour, or until tender, adding salt towards the end of the cooking time. Drain and place in a bowl, ready to be used in this recipe.

+ **Serving suggestions:** Some locals add chips to the wrap, so you may like to include my *Kekikli, Pul Biberli Fırın Patates* (page 174). You may also enjoy making your own flatbreads with my *Balon Ekmek* recipe (page 44).

Kumpir

Turkish-Style Baked Potato with Toppings

Serves 4

Kumpir is a much loved street food, especially in Istanbul – it's our version of jacket potato. The baked potato flesh is mashed with butter and cheese until smooth, which forms the base, and is then topped with an array of fillings. It is delicious, easy to make, versatile and always brings back fond memories of feasting on *kumpir* from the street stalls in Ortaköy, Istanbul, when I was a student. Some of the traditional toppings include chopped olives, cooked corn kernels, pickles, and sliced Turkish cured sausage (*sucuk*). It makes a delicious, satisfying dinner with creamy, crunchy, zingy flavours and textures – a great way to finish up your dips and salads, too. In traditional *kumpir*, the toppings over the baked potato are finished with a squeeze of mayonnaise and ketchup.

4 medium baking potatoes (1 kg/2 lb 4 oz in total)
1½ teaspoons olive oil
sea salt and freshly ground black pepper
1 medium corn on the cob (about 200 g/7 oz)
4 tablespoons salted butter
80 g (3 oz) medium Cheddar cheese, grated

FOR THE QUICK-PICKLED RED CABBAGE
140 g (4½ oz) red cabbage, hard stalks removed and thinly sliced
2 tablespoons cider vinegar or grape vinegar
½ teaspoon sea salt

TOPPING OPTIONS (CAN BE MADE AHEAD)
⅓ x quantity *Kısır* (page 130)
½ x quantity *Cevizli, Yoğurtlu, Sarımsaklı Havuç ve Kabak* (page 102)
½ x quantity *Zeytinli Mantar Sote* (page 104)

TO MAKE THE QUICK-PICKLED RED CABBAGE, combine the sliced cabbage, vinegar and salt in a bowl. With clean fingers, message the salt and vinegar into the cabbage for a minute. Cover and leave in a cool place for at least 1 hour, stirring a few times. You can prepare this ahead and keep covered in the refrigerator for 1–2 weeks in a sealed jar.

Preheat the oven to 200°C fan/220°C/425°F/gas 7.

Clean and dry the potatoes and prick each one in 5–6 places. Rub with a little olive oil and a sprinkle of sea salt and wrap each potato in kitchen foil. Place on a baking sheet and bake on the middle shelf of the oven for 55–60 minutes, turning them around halfway through the cooking time. Remove and discard the foil, then return to the oven to bake for a further 10 minutes until crispy and fully cooked. Using oven gloves, carefully insert a knife to check whether the flesh is tender; if not, cook for another 5–10 minutes. Remove and let cool for a few minutes.

While the potatoes are baking, cut the corn cob crossways and place

in a medium pan. Pour over freshly boiled water to cover and bring back to the boil. Cover and simmer for 10 minutes, or until the corn is cooked. Drain and let cool.

Once cool, place the corn cobs on a chopping board and use a sharp knife to shave off the corn kernels. Place the kernels in a small bowl.

Once the potatoes are cool enough to handle but still hot (the potato flesh needs to be hot to be mashed well, so use an oven glove if necessary), slice each potato lengthways through the middle (take care to not to cut all the way through) and gently open up. Fluff up the potato flesh with a fork then add a tablespoon of butter to each potato, season with salt and pepper to taste and mash really well (take care not to break the potato skin). Divide the grated cheese among the potatoes and mash again until smooth and creamy. Top with your favourite toppings, sprinkle with the corn kernels and some quick-pickled red cabbage (or your choice of chopped pickles) and serve immediately.

Simit

Sesame-Encrusted Turkish Bread Rings

Makes 8

I adore *simit* and it really is the most quintessential Turkish snack. You can have *simit* for breakfast with a cup of *çay* (Turkish tea), sliced cucumber, tomatoes, *beyaz peynir* (our feta) and olives, or you can enjoy them for a mid-morning or afternoon snack. Turks mostly prefer savoury accompaniments to *simit*, although I must say it is also lovely with some butter and jam. *Simit* has always been so widely available that no one really attempted to make it at home, especially while I was growing up. Moving abroad in my late twenties, I greatly missed *simit* and was delighted to come across dear Leanne Kitchen's recipe in her beautiful book, *Turkey: Recipes and Tales From the Road*. I have adapted Leanne's *simit* recipe and have been making *simit* successfully thanks to her for over 13 years. Each time it brings a huge dose of home and joy back to me. It really is easy to make once you get the hang of the shaping – a popular one at my cookery classes.

¼ teaspoon sugar
60 ml (2 fl oz/¼ cup) lukewarm water (1st stage)
1 tablespoon dried yeast
310 ml (10 ¾ fl oz/ generous 1¼ cups) lukewarm water (2nd stage)
500 g (1 lb 2oz/4 cups) plain (all-purpose) flour, plus extra for dusting
2 teaspoons sea salt
olive oil, for greasing

FOR COATING
140 ml (4½ fl oz/generous ½ cup) grape molasses
60 ml (2 fl oz/¼ cup) water
155 g (5 oz/1 cup) sesame seeds

Combine the sugar and 1st stage quantity of lukewarm water in a small bowl, then sprinkle over the dried yeast, and mix well with a small spoon. Set aside for about 8 minutes, or until foamy.

Next add the 2nd stage quantity of lukewarm water to the yeast mixture and combine well.

Combine the flour and salt in a large bowl and make a well in the middle. Pour in the yeast mixture and stir to form a rough dough. Turn out onto a lightly floured surface and knead for about 5 minutes, or until the dough is smooth and elastic. Roll the dough into a ball and place in a lightly oiled bowl, turning to coat. Cover with cling film (plastic wrap) and leave to rise in a warm, draught-free place for 45 minutes–1 hour, or until doubled in size.

Preheat the oven to 200°C fan/220°C/425°F/gas 7 and line 2 large baking sheets with baking paper. For coating, combine the grape molasses with the water in a large bowl and mix well. Place the sesame seeds on a large, flat plate.

Knock back the dough on a lightly floured, clean work surface and divide it into 8 even-sized pieces. Working with one piece of dough at a time, use your hands to roll the dough out to a 60 cm (24 in) rope. Fold in half so the two ends align and twist into a two-stranded rope. Join the ends together to make a circle, pressing firmly to seal and rolling the ends with your palm to make a neat ring shape. Repeat with the remaining dough to make 8 rings.

Dip each ring into the grape molasses mixture, immersing completely to coat, then let any excess drip off into the bowl. Next, toss in the sesame seeds, turning gently to coat both sides. Transfer to the prepared baking sheets and gently stretch to make neat rings. Set aside at room temperature for about 10 minutes until puffed slightly. Bake for 17–18 minutes, or until deep golden and cooked through. Transfer to a wire rack to cool.

+ **Serving suggestions:** Enjoy *simit* with eggs, with *meze*, or as an all-day snack. It is delicious with *Çılbır* (page 61), as well as with Unscrambled *Menemen* (page 62), where you can gently reheat simit pieces in the pan, soaking up the flavours. Also try *simit* with butter and *Kuru İncir Reçeli* (page 242) – it is divine.

+ **Note:** Grape molasses, *üzüm pekmezi*, is traditionally used in making *simit*. If you can't get grape molasses, date, fig or carob molasses would work, too.

Patatesli, Ispanaklı Gözleme

Stuffed Flatbreads with Potato and Spinach

Makes 6

The origin of these stuffed flatbreads goes back thousands of years. Turkish *yörüks* (nomads) made *gözleme* as they travelled from Central Asia and settled in Anatolia, today's mainland *Türkiye* (Turkey). You can find *gözleme* in street stalls, markets and cafés with a variety of fillings offered in each region. It can be enjoyed for breakfast with a cup of *çay*, for lunch or as an all-day wholesome snack. Traditionally cooked over a round *sac* griddle, it is one of the nation's favourite snacks. It is also easy to make at home and versatile - mashed potatoes, cheese, chopped spinach, herbs and sautéed minced (ground) meat are some of the popular fillings. You can use a wide non-stick pan to cook your *gözleme* at home.

450 g (1 lb/generous 3½ cups) plain (all-purpose) flour, sifted, plus extra for dusting
1 teaspoon sea salt
3 tablespoons olive oil, plus a drizzle for oiling
225 ml (8 fl oz/scant 1 cup) lukewarm water
40 g (1½ oz) butter (or plant-based alternative), to spread over cooked *gözleme*

FOR THE FILLING
680 g (1 lb 8 oz) potatoes, peeled and cut into 5 cm (2 in) chunks
1 teaspoon ground cumin
3 tablespoons olive oil
1 medium onion, quartered and thinly sliced
150 g (5 oz) spinach leaves, thinly sliced
½ teaspoon *pul biber*
sea salt and freshly ground black pepper, to taste

Prepare the filling first. Place the potatoes in a medium pan, pour in enough hot water to cover and add a pinch of salt. Bring to the boil, partially cover and simmer over a medium heat for 20 minutes, or until the potatoes are fully cooked. Drain and place in a large mixing bowl to cool for a few minutes, then add the cumin, season with salt and pepper, and mash until smooth.

Heat the olive oil in a large, wide sauté pan over a medium–high heat, add the onion and cook for 10 minutes, stirring often, until softened and golden. Add to the potato mash along with the chopped spinach and *pul biber*. Once cool enough to handle, combine everything with clean hands – this will soften the spinach and blend everything well. Check the seasoning and add more salt or spices to taste, combining well. Cover with cling film (plastic wrap) and set aside.

FOR THE DOUGH, place the flour in a large mixing bowl, make a well in the middle and sprinkle in the salt, add the olive oil and pour in the lukewarm water. With clean hands, combine to a rough dough. On a lightly floured surface, knead the dough for 2–3 minutes to a smooth, semi-firm ball. Place in a bowl, coat with a drizzle of oil and cover with a damp dish towel. Leave to rest for 20 minutes.

Place the rested dough on a lightly floured surface and divide into 6 equal pieces. Roll each piece into a ball and place them back in the bowl, covered with the damp towel to keep them moist. Take one dough ball out at a time and use a rolling pin to roll out to a thin circle (about 27 cm/11 in in diameter and 1 mm/1/16 in thick). Spread a sixth of the filling (about 6 heaped tablespoons) evenly over one half of the circle, leaving 2 cm (¾ in) around the edges clear. Fold the dough over to enclose the filling and make a half-moon shape. Gently pat the top of the *gözleme* to get rid of any air bubbles and press down the edges with your fingers to seal well. Place on a tray side by side and cover with a clean towel so it won't dry out. Repeat with the rest of the dough balls and filling.

Heat a large, wide non-stick pan over a high heat. Place a *gözleme* in the pan and cook for 1 minute, then carefully flip over and cook the other side for another minute. Flip again and cook for about 45 seconds (light brown circles will start to appear). Flip over again and cook for about 45 seconds. By now the *gözleme* should be cooked with visible light brown patches on the surface. Place the cooked *gözleme* on a clean tray side by side and spread butter on both sides. Cover with a clean towel to keep moist and cook the rest of the *gözleme* in the same way. Serve warm or at room temperature.

+ **Prepare ahead:** You can make the filling a day ahead and
  keep covered in the refrigerator. You can also use leftover
  mashed potatoes or your choice of filling. *Gözleme* can
  be made a day ahead and kept covered in the fridge, too.
  Simply reheat in a non-stick pan over medium to high
  heat for about 1½ minutes each side.

Sokak Yemekleri

Nohutlu Pilav

Pilaf with Chickpeas

Serves 4-6

Buttery *Nohutlu Pilav* dates back to the Ottoman palace kitchens. Mehmed the Conqueror's Grand Vizier, Mahmut Pasha, would serve *Nohutlu Pilav* to his guests, hiding pieces of chickpea-sized gold in the pilaf. Whoever found the gold could keep it as the Vizier's gift. An easy, comforting pilaf, and one of my children's favourites, too.

370 g (13 oz/generous 1¾ cups) long-grain rice

55 g (2 oz) salted butter (or plant-based alternative)

400 g (14 oz) tin pre-cooked chickpeas (garbanzo beans), drained and rinsed (discard any loose skins)

sea salt and freshly ground black pepper, to taste

560 ml (19 fl oz/2¼ cups) hot water

Place the rice in a strainer and rinse under warm running water for a couple of minutes until the water runs clear – this helps to get rid of the excess starch and keeps the rice grains separate (*tane tane pilav*, as we say in Turkish). Drain the excess liquid.

Melt the butter in a medium pan over a low heat and stir in the rinsed rice to coat the grains with the butter. Sauté for a minute, then add the cooked chickpeas, season with salt and pepper, and combine well. Pour in the hot water, cover and bring to the boil, then reduce to a simmer for 18–20 minutes until all the liquid is absorbed. Turn the heat off, cover the pan with 2 sturdy paper towels, place the lid back on top and leave the rice to rest for 10 minutes (the paper towels will absorb any excess moisture).

Fluff up the rice and check the seasoning, then serve.

+ **Note:** If you are using dried chickpeas, you need to soak them in cold water overnight, drain and put them in a pan with plenty of fresh water. Cook for about 1 hour, or until tender, adding salt toward the end of the cooking time. Drain and set aside.

+ **Serving suggestion:** *Nohutlu Pilav* is a meal in itself with a refreshing salad such as *Karışık Mevsim Salatası* (page 124) or pickles on the side.

Kekikli, Pul Biberli Fırın Patates

Baked Potato Chips with Pul Biber and Oregano

Serves 4-6

These baked potato chips certainly bring back happy childhood memories. Rather than at street vendors, you enjoy them fried at our traditional no-frills *esnaf lokantası* (restaurants) as well as kebab shops. My mother would bake *Fırın Patates* and serve along with her *Şakşuka* (page 108) and her signature *Muhammara* (page 97). A heavenly combination.

1 kg (2 lb 4 oz) Maris Piper or similar baking potatoes
3 tablespoons olive oil
¾ teaspoon sea salt (use less if you prefer)
½ teaspoon *pul biber* (add more if you enjoy heat!)
1 teaspoon dried oregano

Preheat the oven to 200°C fan/220°C/425°F/gas 7.

Wash the potatoes and dry thoroughly, then cut into 1.5 cm (⅔ in) thick chips. Thoroughly pat the chips dry and spread over a large baking sheet in one layer. Drizzle the olive oil over the chips and sprinkle with the salt, *pul biber* and dried oregano. Use your hands to toss the chips in the oil and seasoning, then arrange them again in one layer and not touching one another, so that they can crisp up around the edges.

Bake for 35-40 minutes, turning the chips halfway through the cooking time, until golden brown and crispy. Serve immediately while hot.

+ Leftovers: Use the leftover baked chips in *Patatesli Yumurta* (page 64).

Pilav, Bulgurlu, Mercimekli Tatlar

Eight Wholegrains, Pulses and Rice

Pilav, Bulgurlu, Mercimekli Tatlar

Wholegrains, pulses and rice are an essential part of the Turkish diet – Anatolia, mainland *Türkiye* (Turkey), is regarded as the 'home of wheat', as wheat has been cultivated here for almost 10,000 years. Bulgur is a grain from cooked wheat berries, which have the bran removed and are then dried and pounded. I adore the nutty texture of bulgur and its benefits are numerous – high in fibre, low in fat and rich in protein and minerals. We often combine bulgur with vegetables and flavour with spices, herbs and natural condiments, such as pomegranate molasses, as in the very moreish *Mercimekli, Bulgurlu Köfte* (page 180). Freekeh is another popular ancient grain – a superfood that is harvested before it is ripened, its smoky flavour is fantastic combined with vegetables and pulses. I highly recommend *Pancarlı Nar Ekşili, Firik* (page 185) – it is one of my favourite recipes and a good way to repurpose any leftovers of *Nar Ekşili, Cevizli Pancar* (page 92).

I love the variety of ways that Turkish cuisine incorporates grains, rice and pulses into wholesome meals that are packed with flavour. Please do try the fragrant *Kestaneli İç Pilav* (page 189), it is a taste sensation with chestnuts, juicy apricots and refreshing dill – easy to make and impressive to serve.

Mercimekli, Bulgurlu Köfte

Bulgur and Lentil Patties

Serves 4

These delicious, great value and wholesome bulgur and lentil patties are a real crowd pleaser – you can serve them wrapped in lettuce leaves with a squeeze of lemon juice or drizzle of pomegranate molasses. Sautéed onions are important here, as they add oodles of flavour and moisture to the patties. This recipe was passed down to my mother from her neighbours when we lived in Elazığ, a city at the southeast part of the country, where these delicious patties were served at ladies' afternoon gatherings. I remember the locals being very warm and friendly, always happy to share their food.

2 tablespoons olive oil, plus an extra drizzle

2 medium onions, finely chopped

1 tablespoon double concentrated tomato paste

1 tablespoon Turkish red pepper paste (*biber salçası*, see page 218 for homemade)

200 g (7 oz/generous ¾ cup) red lentils, rinsed

500 ml (17 fl oz/2 cups) hot water (for the lentils)

130 g (4 oz/¾ cup) fine bulgur

200 ml (7 fl oz/scant 1 cup) hot water (for the fine bulgur)

4 spring onions (scallions), trimmed and finely chopped

small bunch of flat-leaf parsley, finely chopped

1½ teaspoons ground cumin

1 teaspoon *pul biber* or red pepper flakes (optional)

1–1¼ teaspoons sea salt (use less if you wish) and freshly ground black pepper, to taste

small lettuce leaves, to serve

lemon wedges or a drizzle of pomegranate molasses (*nar ekşisi*, see page 220 for homemade), to serve

Heat the 2 tablespoons of olive oil in a wide sauté pan over a medium–high heat, add the onions and sauté for 10–12 minutes, stirring often until softened and starting to caramelise. Add the tomato paste and red pepper paste, and combine well, then set aside to cool.

Place the rinsed red lentils in a medium saucepan with 500 ml (17 fl oz/2 cups) hot water. Bring to the boil, then reduce to a simmer for about 15 minutes until fully cooked. Remove any scum that rises to the surface with a spoon and stir occasionally so that the lentils don't stick to the bottom of the pan. Drain off any leftover liquid – the cooked lentils will be the consistency of a thick purée. Set aside to cool in a large bowl.

In the same pan, combine the bulgur with 200 ml (7 fl oz/scant 1 cup) hot water, cover and let the bulgur absorb the water for 5 minutes.

Combine the cooked bulgur with the lentils, and add the sautéed onions, spring onions and parsley. Stir in the ground cumin, *pul biber* (if using), and salt and pepper (the mixture needs a good seasoning; adjust the salt to your taste).

Set a bowl of room-temperature water with a drizzle of olive oil near you. Slightly dampen your hands and knead the bulgur and lentil mixture for a couple of minutes until well combined – it will be a soft dough consistency. Check the seasoning and add more salt or spices to your taste, then mix well. Dampen your hands and take a large walnut-sized piece of the mixture and shape it into a patty. Place on a wide serving plate over a bed of lettuce leaves. Repeat to use up all the mixture.

Serve with lemon wedges on the side or with a drizzle of pomegranate molasses, as my husband prefers.

+ **Prepare ahead:** These patties keep well in the refrigerator, covered, for 2–3 days.

+ **Serving suggestions:** These patties accompany *Turkish Şakşuka* (page 108) as well as pickles beautifully. The Turkish red pepper paste, *biber salçası*, adds a wonderful depth of flavour to these patties – you can make your own with my recipe on page 218.

Sebzeli Bulgur Pilavı

Bulgur Pilaf with Aubergines, Peppers and Tomatoes

Serves 4-6

This is a really lovely dish, a meal in itself. Traditionally, aubergines (eggplant) and peppers are finely diced here, though I love their texture and keep them on the chunky side. I also prefer to bake them rather than frying – lighter and equally delicious. This is especially enjoyed during the summer at home, when the aubergine, peppers and tomatoes are in abundance. If you can get ripe tomatoes, you can dice them to use instead of tinned. The cooling cucumber and yoghurt dip (*Cacık*) complements this dish beautifully.

2 medium aubergines (eggplant), trimmed
sea salt and freshly ground black pepper, to taste
6 tablespoons olive oil
1 green and 1 red (bell) pepper
1 medium onion, finely sliced
1 tablespoon double concentrated tomato paste
400 g (14 oz) tin chopped tomatoes
400 g (14 oz/2¼ cups) coarse bulgur, rinsed
460 ml (16 fl oz/1¾ cups) hot water
1 teaspoon *pul biber*
1 teaspoon dried mint

FOR THE CACIK DIP
150 g (5 oz) cucumber, diced
275 g (10 oz/generous 1 cup) plain yoghurt (or plant-based alternative)
dried mint, to sprinkle
sea salt, to taste

Preheat the oven to 200°C fan/220°C/425°F/gas 7.

Cut the aubergines lengthways in quarters and then slice into 1 cm (½ in) pieces. Lay them on a baking sheet and sprinkle salt over them, and set aside for 10 minutes (salt will help the moisture and bitter juices come out of the aubergine).

Dry the aubergines and baking sheet thoroughly with sturdy paper towels and spread the aubergines in one layer. Pour over 3 tablespoons of the olive oil and use your hands to coat well. Bake for 20 minutes.

Cut the peppers in half, deseed and remove the hard stalk. Cut each half into 3 wedges and slice each wedge into 1 cm (½ in) chunks. When the aubergines have had 20 minutes in the oven, remove and stir in the chopped peppers. Pour over 2 tablespoons of olive oil, season with salt and pepper, and bake for a further 20 minutes until the vegetables start to char at the edges. Remove from the oven and set aside.

Heat the remaining 1 tablespoon of oil in a large pan over a medium heat, add the onion and sauté for 5 minutes until softened. Stir in the tomato paste and chopped tomatoes, and bring to a gentle boil. Stir in the rinsed bulgur and combine well, then pour in the hot water, season with *pul biber*, salt and pepper, and mix well. Cover and cook over a low heat for about 15 minutes, or until the bulgur has absorbed all the liquid. Turn the heat off, cover the pan with a clean dish towel and place the lid on firmly. Rest the pilaf for 10 minutes (the towel will absorb excess moisture).

Gently combine the baked aubergine and peppers with the bulgur, stir in the dried mint and combine well.

FOR THE CACIK DIP, simply combine the diced cucumbers with the yoghurt in a bowl. Sprinkle over some dried mint, season with salt to taste and mix well. Serve on the side of the pilaf.

+ **Prepare ahead and tips:** Leftovers keep well in the refrigerator for 2-3 days, great to prepare ahead. If preferred, you can use rice instead of bulgur, and include chopped dill, as it is enjoyed in the Aegean region, which will make this dish gluten-free, too.

Pancarlı Nar Ekşili, Firik

Freekeh with Beetroot and Pomegranate Molasses

Serves 4

This is one of my favourite recipes in this book and my own creation, showcasing much-loved pomegranate molasses and freekeh in the south. Freekeh is an ancient grain, made from green durum wheat, and it is a superfood, often combined with vegetables and bulgur in Turkish cuisine. Tangy pomegranate molasses dressing and spring onions (scallions) add a touch of freshness, along with the pomegranate seeds. I love the sweetness from baked beets in this recipe – you can bake the beets with garlic as in my recipe for *Nar Ekşili, Cevizli Pancar* (page 92) to use here. If pressed for time, you can use pre-cooked beets, too.

2 tablespoons olive oil

1 medium onion, finely chopped

130 g (4 oz/¾ cup) freekeh, rinsed and drained

340 ml (12 fl oz/scant 1½ cups) hot water

sea salt and freshly ground black pepper, to taste

280 g (10 oz) pre-cooked (or baked) beetroot (beets), sliced into bite-size chunks

3 spring onions (scallions), finely chopped

small bunch of flat-leaf parsley, finely chopped

FOR THE POMEGRANATE MOLASSES SAUCE

1 tablespoon pomegranate molasses (*nar ekşisi*, see page 220 for homemade)

1 tablespoon water

2 tablespoons extra-virgin olive oil

sea salt and freshly ground black pepper, to taste

TO SERVE

85 g (3 oz) crumbled *beyaz peynir* or feta (or chopped, pitted olives or plant-based cheese)

85 g (3 oz) pomegranate seeds

Heat the olive oil in a medium pan over a medium heat, add the onion and sauté for 8 minutes until softened and beginning to colour. Stir in the rinsed freekeh and combine well for a minute. Pour in the hot water, season with salt and pepper, and mix well. Cover and cook for 25–30 minutes over a low heat, until all the liquid is absorbed. Turn the heat off, cover the pan with a clean dish towel and place the lid on firmly. Rest for 10 minutes (the towel will absorb excess moisture).

FOR THE POMEGRANATE MOLASSES SAUCE, combine the pomegranate molasses, water and oil in a small bowl. Season with salt and pepper, and combine well.

Stir the cooked freekeh and place on a large serving dish. Add the cooked beetroot, spring onions and parsley, and pour over the pomegranate molasses sauce. Gently combine well using a serving spoon. Crumble over the *beyaz peynir* or feta (or plant-based option), sprinkle with the pomegranate seeds and serve.

+ **Serving suggestion:** You can pair this with *Öcce* fritters (page 110) for a delicious meal.

Taze Fasulyeli Bulgur Pilavı

Bulgur Pilaf with Green Beans, Onions and Tomatoes

Serves 4-6

Green beans cooked in olive oil, (*Zeytinyağlı Taze Fasulye*) is a popular dish at home. My mother would often add bulgur to the leftovers of it to make this delicious pilaf. I love nutty bulgur combined with vegetables this way, for easy, good-value and wholesome weekday suppers. Runner beans are traditionally used, although French dwarf beans would work well, too.

350 g (12 oz) runner beans or French dwarf beans
2 tablespoons olive oil
1 onion, finely chopped
4 garlic cloves, finely chopped
400 g (14 oz) tin chopped tomatoes
225 ml (8 fl oz/scant 1 cup) hot water (for the beans)
sea salt and freshly ground black pepper, to taste
400 g (14 oz/2¼ cups) coarse bulgur, rinsed
1 teaspoon *pul biber*, or to taste
340 ml (12 fl oz/1½ cups) hot water (for the bulgur)
plain yoghurt (or plant-based alternative), to serve

Rinse and trim the runner beans, cut lengthways, then slice into 7 cm (3 in) long strips (if French dwarf beans are used, no need to slice lengthways). Place in a bowl and set aside.

Heat the olive oil in a medium pan over a medium heat, add the onion and sauté for 5 minutes, stirring often. Stir in the beans and garlic, and combine for a minute. Add the chopped tomatoes and 225 ml (8 fl oz/scant 1 cup) hot water, season with salt and pepper, and mix well. Cover and bring to the boil, then reduce to a simmer for 25 minutes. The beans will soften but will still have a bite to them at the end of this time.

Stir in the rinsed bulgur, *pul biber* and 340 ml (12 fl oz/1½ cups) hot water, combine well, then cover and cook over a low heat for 15 minutes until all the liquid is absorbed. Turn the heat off, cover the pan with a clean dish towel and place the lid on firmly. Rest for 10 minutes (the towel will absorb excess moisture).

Fluff the pilaf, check the seasoning, adding more salt, pepper or *pul biber* to your taste. Serve hot with a dollop of plain yoghurt (or a plant-based alternative) on the side.

+ **Prepare ahead:** This is a generous dish and leftovers are lovely the next day, cold or at room temperature.

+ **Serving suggestions:** Pickles such as *Salatalık Turşusu* (page 217) or *Pancar ve Şalgam Turşusu* (page 216) go well with this dish, too.

Pilav, Bulgurlu, Mercimekli Tatlar

Kestaneli İç Pilav

Rice Pilaf with Chestnuts, Apricots and Herbs

Serves 6-8

This fragrant, festive pilaf is a specialty from the Ottoman palace kitchens and absolutely scrumptious. It encapsulates different textures and flavours – there are the earthy chestnuts and pine nuts, juicy apricots and currants, refreshing dill and parsley with a touch of lemon, and they complement one another beautifully. Although there are many versions of *İç Pilav*, the common feature is that it always has dried fruits and nuts in it, a legacy from the Ottoman period. *Kestaneli İç Pilav* appears on our tables on special occasions, religious festivities and for New Year's Eve. Short-grain baldo rice is traditionally used at home, although long-grain or basmati rice work well, too. It is impressive to serve and a meal in itself with a refreshing salad and/or pickles on the side.

2 tablespoons currants
350 g (12 oz/1¾ cups) long-grain rice
2 tablespoons salted **butter** (use olive or vegetable oil instead for a plant-based option)
2 tablespoons olive oil
1 medium onion, finely chopped
3 tablespoons pine nuts
170 g (6 oz) dried apricots, quartered
170 g (6 oz) cooked chestnuts, chopped into small bite-size pieces
2 teaspoons ground cinnamon (or more to taste)
sea salt and freshly ground black pepper, to taste
770 ml (27 fl oz/generous 3 cups) hot water
small bunch of flat-leaf parsley, finely chopped
small bunch of dill, hard stalks removed, finely chopped
1 tablespoon fresh lemon juice

Soak the currants in warm water for 15 minutes, then drain and set aside. Also soak the rice in a bowl of warm water for 10 minutes, then drain and rinse under cold running water until the water runs clear. This helps to get rid of the extra starch and keep the rice grains separate.

Heat the butter and olive oil in a heavy, medium pan over a medium heat, add the onion and cook for 7–8 minutes until softened, stirring often. Add the pine nuts and sauté for about 2 minutes, stirring continuously. As they begin to turn golden, stir in the currants, apricots, chestnuts, cinnamon and the rinsed rice, and combine well for a minute. Season with salt and pepper, pour in the hot water and bring to the boil, then reduce the heat, cover and simmer gently for 18–20 minutes, or until all the liquid has been absorbed. Turn the heat off, cover the pan with a clean dish towel and place the lid on firmly. Rest for 10 minutes (the towel will absorb excess moisture).

Stir in the chopped parsley, dill and lemon juice, and combine gently, ready to serve and enjoy.

+ **Serving suggestions:** Serve warm with pickles and a refreshing salad such as *Bostana Salatası* (page 127) on the side. Leftovers are delicious cold or at room temperature the next day, too.

Ocak ve Fırın Yemekleri

Nine

Casseroles, Stews and Pasta

Ocak ve Fırın Yemekleri

Turkish stews and casseroles are the ultimate comfort food, as well as being nutritious, versatile and easy to make. Combining nuts, pulses and seasonal produce, there's something delicious for everyone in this chapter. Try our iconic bean stew, *Kuru Fasulye* (page 199), comforting and great value too. I feel most readers will also be joyous to discover *Fırında Patates Paçası* (page 208) – humble, scrumptious, garlicky mashed potatoes in the Turkish way, which can be paired with many recipes in this book. Many dishes in this chapter conveniently freeze well and I encourage you to experiment and use whatever ingredients you have to hand.

This chapter also pays tribute to one of the nation's favourites: *Mantı,* our historic dumplings, along with other pasta-based delights. I hope you enjoy making the showstopper *Nohutlu Tepsi Mantısı* (page 204), a regional specialty with a spiced chickpea (garbanzo bean) filling – a practical feast too as it can be prepared ahead.

Fırında Sebzeli, Nohutlu Türlü

Baked Vegetables with Chickpeas

Serves 6-8

I love the abundance of seasonal vegetables (*sebze*) we get at home. This is a wonderful bake that celebrates that bounty. *Türlü* is traditionally cooked on the stovetop as a stew, although I prefer to bake it in the oven as I love the additional layer of flavours baking brings. It is worth turning the oven on, as it is a generous dish and freezes well. Chickpeas (garbanzo beans) in a casserole are typical Turkish fare – their earthy flavour goes well with the vegetables in this versatile all-in-one dish. In winter months, you can use root vegetables, such as beetroot (beets) and potatoes, or even squash, leeks, etc.

3 medium aubergines (eggplant), trimmed, halved lengthways and sliced into 1 cm (½ in) chunks (halve larger chunks)
sea salt and freshly ground black pepper, to taste
3 medium courgettes (zucchini), trimmed, halved lengthways and sliced into 1 cm (½ in) chunks
2 medium carrots, trimmed, halved lengthways and sliced into 1 cm (½ in) chunks
2 medium red onions, roughly chopped
1 green and 1 red (bell) pepper, deseeded and roughly chopped
4 tablespoons olive oil
1 tablespoon dried oregano
2 teaspoons *pul biber* or red pepper flakes
6 garlic cloves, roughly chopped
400 g (14 oz) tin chopped tomatoes
400 g (14 oz) tin pre-cooked chickpeas (garbanzo beans), drained and rinsed (discard any loose skins)
2 teaspoons ground cumin
300 ml (10 fl oz/1¼ cups) hot water
1 tablespoon double concentrated tomato paste

Preheat the oven to 200°C fan/220°C/425°F/gas 7.

Spread the aubergine slices on a wide tray, sprinkle with salt and set aside for about 10 minutes. Using paper towels, gently squeeze the excess moisture out of the aubergines.

In a large lipped baking sheet, toss all the vegetables, apart from the garlic, with the olive oil, oregano, *pul biber*/red pepper flakes, and some salt and pepper. Use your hands to ensure all the vegetables are well coated – this really helps enhance their flavour. Bake for about 40 minutes, turning the vegetables around halfway through, until charred at the edges and softened.

Remove from the oven and transfer the vegetables to a large, deep baking dish, about 27 × 15 cm (11 × 6 in). Stir in the chopped garlic, chopped tomatoes, chickpeas and cumin, season with salt and pepper, and combine well. Use the empty tomato tin to combine the hot water with the tomato paste and mix well. Pour this into the baking dish and gently combine. Check the seasoning and add more salt and pepper to your taste.

Bake for 30-35 minutes until all vegetables are cooked through, browned at the edges, and the sauce has thickened. Serve immediately.

+ **Prepare ahead:** You can roast the vegetables ahead of time. Or the whole dish can actually be made in advance, as the flavours settle and it tastes even better the next day.

+ **Leftovers:** Crack an egg or two over leftovers for another delicious, easy supper.

+ **Serving suggestions:** You can serve as it is with crusty bread or plain rice. I also love to spread this wholesome *Türlü* over *Beğendi* (page 221). Please note that this meal won't be vegan in that case.

Hellimli Sebzeli Kebap

Aubergine, Courgette and Halloumi Bake

Serves 4-6

I am often asked for a vegetarian alternative to my popular Aubergine Kebab with Meatballs and so I came up with this delicious version, which is a huge hit with my family (not all kebabs are skewered; some are layered on a tray and baked, like this one). I love the firm texture and robust, salty taste of Cypriot halloumi (*hellim*). Even though it is not traditional kebab fare, we do use halloumi in the modern Turkish kitchen. Here, the meaty, naturally sweet aubergines (eggplant) melt in the mouth and the firm, salty halloumi works perfectly, keeping its shape and texture, as it has a high melting point.

2 medium, long aubergines (eggplant), trimmed and sliced into 1½ cm (½ in) discs

1 medium courgette (zucchini), trimmed and sliced into 1½ cm (½ in) discs

sea salt and freshly ground black pepper, to taste

4 tablespoons olive oil

1 green (bell) pepper, trimmed, deseeded, cut lengthways in wedges and sliced into 1 cm (½ in) strips

350 g (12 oz) halloumi, drained, patted dry and cut into slices 1 cm (½ in) thick

1 medium tomato, sliced into 1 cm (½ in) discs

85 ml (3 fl oz/scant 6 tablespoons) water

FOR THE SAUCE
3 garlic cloves, finely chopped
3 tablespoons water
1 tablespoon olive oil
2 tablespoons double concentrated tomato paste
1 teaspoon dried mint
1 teaspoon *pul biber*
sea salt and freshly ground black pepper, to taste

Preheat the oven to 200°C fan/220°C/425°F/gas 7.

Spread the aubergine and courgette slices over a large tray, sprinkle with a little salt and set aside for 10 minutes.

Gently pat the aubergine and courgette slices with paper towels to squeeze out their excess moisture, then transfer to a large lipped baking sheet. Pour over 3 tablespoons of olive oil, season with salt and pepper, and use your hands to ensure everything is well coated. Arrange in one layer, then bake for 15 minutes.

Remove from the oven and turn the vegetables around. Stir in the peppers and gently coat with the remaining olive oil and bake for a further 10 minutes until charred at the edges and softened.

Meanwhile, pat the halloumi slices with a paper towel to ensure they are well dried, and set aside.

FOR THE SAUCE, combine all the ingredients in a small bowl, season with salt and pepper, and mix well. Brush the sauce over both sides of the baked vegetables.

In a 20 cm (8 in) baking dish, stack the vegetables upright, side by side, alternating between aubergines and courgettes, and tucking the halloumi and fresh tomato slices in between, ensuring they all stay upright quite tightly. Gently insert the peppers in between the vegetable and halloumi slices. Pour the water into the remaining sauce to loosen and combine well, then drizzle over the dish. Cover and bake for 25 minutes, then uncover and bake for another 12–15 minutes, or until the halloumi slices are golden. Serve immediately.

+ **Prepare ahead and variations:** You can par-bake the vegetables ahead of time, then combine with the halloumi and bake further, just before eating. To make this a vegan dinner, you can use vegan halloumi or leave the cheese out altogether. Instead, try sliced portobello mushrooms or more aubergine/courgettes (zucchini).

+ **Serving suggestion:** Serve this delicious bake with *Haydari* (page 98) and *Nohutlu Pilav* (page 173) for a complete meal.

Kuru Fasulye

Turkish Dried Bean Stew

Serves 6

One of our national dishes and served with rice, referred to as *kuru fasulye-pilav*, this is one of the most iconic comfort foods you will find served at our traditional, no-frills, buffet-style *esnaf lokantası* and at home. It was a firm favourite of my dear belated father, Orhan. There are many variations of this delicious bean stew and almost every household has their own version. Cubed lamb, beef, Turkish spicy sausage (*sucuk*) or dried cured beef (*pastırma*) can be added, too, although I absolutely love the vegetarian version here – for us, the beans slowly cooked with onions and green peppers are so delicious that we don't miss the meat.

350 g (12 oz/1¾ cups) dried cannellini or haricot beans

60 ml (2 fl oz/¼ cup) olive oil

2 medium onions, finely diced

1 green (bell) pepper or 2 green Turkish pointed peppers, diced

1 tablespoon double concentrated tomato paste

1 tablespoon Turkish red pepper paste (*biber salçası*, see page 218 for homemade)

660 ml (23 fl oz/2¾ cups) water

sea salt and freshly ground black pepper, to taste

1 teaspoon *pul biber* or red pepper flakes (optional)

Soak the dried beans overnight (or for at least 8 hours) in plenty of cold water. The next day, drain the beans, place in a large saucepan and cover with plenty of fresh, cold water. Bring to the boil, then cook over a low–medium heat for 30 minutes, stirring often and skimming off the foam forming on top with a spoon, until partially cooked and still firm, with a bite to them. Drain and set aside in a bowl.

Heat the olive oil in the same pan over a medium heat, add the onions and sauté for 8 minutes until softening and starting to colour around the edges. Add the peppers and sauté for 5 minutes, then add the tomato paste, pepper paste and the beans and combine well for a minute. Pour in the water, season with salt and pepper, and mix well. Bring to the boil then reduce to a simmer, cover and cook for 55–60 minutes until the beans are tender. Taste and add more seasoning if you like; stir in the *pul biber* if you enjoy extra heat. Rest the stew for 10 minutes, then serve hot.

+ **Prepare ahead:** Easy to make in advance – it is even more delicious the next day, as the flavours develop.

+ **Quick option:** Dried beans work best in this stew, but if you can only get pre-cooked tinned beans, use the best quality you can. It's a delicious, wholesome way to enjoy beans in no time. Gently fold 2 x 400 g (14 oz) tins of pre-cooked, drained and rinsed cannellini beans into the sautéed onion, pepper, tomato and pepper paste, add the water and seasoning, and simmer for about 20 minutes.

+ **Serving suggestions:** Plain rice or *Nohutlu Pilav* (page 173) as well as pickles (such as *Salatalık Turşusu*, page 217) are the traditional accompaniment to *Kuru Fasulye*. Or simply enjoy it with chunks of bread for a hearty, comforting meal.

Ekşili Nohutlu Bamya

Okra with Chickpeas, Lemon and Dried Mint

Serves 4

In my hometown of Antakya, we would not only enjoy fresh okra in summer but also dried okra later in the year. There are many ways to enjoy okra throughout *Türkiye* (Turkey); as stew, flavoured with lemon juice; as a soup in central Anatolia; and in some regions meat is added. In the south, okra is combined with earthy chickpeas (garbanzo beans) for a substantial meal. *Sumak ekşisi* (sumac juice made from crushed sumac berries in water) can also be used to intensify the sour taste. With our southern Turkish heritage, this is how my mother would cook okra, with plenty of lemon juice, extra tang from ground sumac and freshness from dried mint (a must for us as it elevates the taste and works well with the sour sauce). I absolutely adore this humble, delicious, wholesome dish that is so easy to make. It's not always easy to get fresh okra, although frozen okra is readily available and works very well.

450 g (1 lb) fresh or frozen okra

2 tablespoons olive oil

1 large onion, finely chopped

4 garlic cloves, finely chopped

400 g (14 oz) tin chopped tomatoes

400 g (14 oz) tin pre-cooked chickpeas (garbanzo beans), drained and rinsed (discard any loose skins)

juice of 1 medium lemon

sea salt and freshly ground black pepper, to taste

230 ml (8 fl oz/scant 1 cup) water

1 tablespoon dried mint

½ teaspoon ground sumac (we like this meal quite sour; use more or less to your taste)

bread or plain rice, to serve

If using fresh okra, wash, gently pat dry and only trim the hard top stem without cutting the pod itself, so that the okra won't be slimy during cooking (keep the okra whole).

Heat the olive oil in a large pan over a medium heat, add the onion and sauté for 5 minutes, stirring often. Add the garlic and sauté for 2 minutes, then stir in the chopped tomatoes, chickpeas, lemon juice and okra, season with salt and pepper, and combine well. Swirl the measured water in the tomato tin to get any remaining bits and pour into the pan. Gently combine, cover and bring to the boil, then reduce to a simmer for 25–30 minutes until the okra is cooked but still firm, not mushy. Gently stir only a few times so that the okra remain whole. Stir in the dried mint and sumac, gently combine well and remove from the heat.

Let the stew rest for 10 minutes, then serve with chunks of bread or plain rice on the side.

+ **Note:** If you are using a string of dried okra, place it in hot water and simmer for 2 minutes until the okra is just soft enough to slip off the string. Drain and remove the string, then the okra is ready to use.

Ocak ve Fırın Yemekleri

Sebzeli, Mercimekli Lazanya

Aubergine, Lentil and Pepper Lasagne

Serves 6-8

I am often asked for a good lasagne recipe, so I am sharing my family's favourite. The filling here is based on Antakya's delicious dish *Mercimekli Mualla* (aubergines/eggplant, lentils and peppers cooked in olive oil). The meaty aubergines, sweet peppers and earthy lentils, not to mention the caramelised onions, make a scrumptious filling. It takes a bit of time to make but it is a generous dish and you can keep leftovers in the freezer, as it reheats beautifully. A comforting crowd pleaser. Use up any other vegetables you have to hand for the filling – courgettes (zucchini), for instance, would be a good option.

2 medium aubergines (eggplant), trimmed, halved lengthways and sliced into 1 cm (½ in) half moons (cut larger pieces in half)

sea salt and freshly ground black pepper, to taste

5 tablespoons olive oil

200 g (7 oz/generous 1 cup) green lentils, rinsed

2 medium onions, thinly sliced

1 red (bell) pepper, deseeded and finely chopped

4 garlic cloves, finely chopped

400 g (14 oz) tin chopped tomatoes

200 ml (7 fl oz/scant 1 cup) water

2 teaspoons dried mint

100 g (3½ oz) butter, cubed

85 g (3 oz/¾ cup) plain (all-purpose) flour

750 ml (25 fl oz/3 cups) warm whole milk

250 g (9 oz) medium Cheddar, grated

11 dried lasagne sheets (about 200 g/7 oz)

Preheat the oven to 200°C fan/220°C/425°F/gas 7.

Place the sliced aubergines on a large lipped baking sheet, sprinkle with salt and leave for 10 minutes. Using sturdy paper towels, gently squeeze out the excess moisture from the aubergine slices. Wipe out any excess salt and moisture on the baking sheet and place them back on the baking sheet and drizzle with 3 tablespoons of the olive oil. Toss with your hands until well coated, then arrange in one layer. Bake in the oven for 20-25 minutes, or until softened and lightly browned. Remove from the oven and set aside.

Meanwhile, place the lentils in a medium saucepan and cover with plenty of hot water. Add a pinch of salt, partially cover and cook for 25 minutes, stirring occasionally, over a medium-low heat. Drain and set aside.

Heat the remaining 2 tablespoons of olive oil in a large pan over a medium heat, add the onions and sauté for 8 minutes, stirring regularly. Add the peppers and sauté for 4 minutes, then stir in the garlic, aubergines and lentils. Add the chopped tomatoes and measured water (pour the water into the tomato tin to use up any leftover bits), add the dried mint and season with salt and pepper. Bring to a gentle simmer and cook for 10 minutes, stirring occasionally. Remove from the heat and set aside.

TO MAKE THE CHEESE SAUCE, melt the butter in a large pan over a medium heat, add the flour and whisk to combine, then pour in the warm milk and whisk constantly until the sauce is thickened, about 6-7 minutes. Add two-thirds of the grated cheese and mix well. Season with pepper and salt (if needed). Remove from the heat.

Preheat the oven to 180°C fan/200°C/400°F/gas 6.

Spread about a third of the filling over the base of a deep 15 × 27 cm (6 × 11 in) baking dish. Cover with a single layer of dried lasagne (about 3½ sheets should do it). Spoon over another third of the filling and add a second layer of lasagne. Pour over half of the cheese sauce and spread roughly, then top with the remaining filling, spreading gently. Add the last layer of lasagne sheets (4 sheets for good coverage) and spread the rest of the cheese sauce over. Sprinkle the remaining grated cheese over the top.

Bake for 35-40 minutes until the topping is golden brown and bubbling. Set aside for 10 minutes for the lasagne to settle, then slice to serve.

Nohutlu Tepsi Mantısı

Baked Mantı Boats with Spiced Chickpeas

Serves 6–8

The word *mantı* derives from *mantou* (Chinese) or *mandu* (Korean), meaning 'dumplings'. We Turks adore *mantı*, which are filled dumplings, and we have many regional varieties. It is a shared culinary heritage that the nomadic Turkish tribes brought with them when they travelled from Central Asia towards Anatolia in the 11th century. Traditionally, family members gather to prepare *mantı* together at home. I have fond memories of being part of these rituals with my grandmother and parents in Istanbul, with the constant flow of tea, coffee and daily gossip. Meat-filled *mantı* are most common, but we also make vegetarian versions. This boat-shaped variety is a specialty of the Bilecik region in northwestern Anatolia, with a delicious spiced chickpea (garbanzo bean) filling. It is baked in the oven and suitable for preparing ahead, which makes it an achievable, impressive centrepiece to share. The marriage of these melt-in-the-mouth *mantı* boats with garlic yoghurt and spice-infused olive oil is simply irresistible.

300 g (10½ oz/scant 2½ cups) plain (all-purpose) flour, plus extra for dusting
1 teaspoon sea salt
1 medium egg, beaten
120 ml (4 fl oz/½ cup) water
2 tablespoons olive oil, plus extra for greasing

FOR THE FILLING
3 tablespoons olive oil
1 medium onion, very finely chopped
small bunch of flat-leaf parsley, finely chopped
400 g (14 oz) tin pre-cooked chickpeas (garbanzo beans), drained and rinsed
1½ teaspoons ground cumin
1 teaspoon *pul biber*
sea salt and freshly ground black pepper, to taste

FOR THE GARLIC YOGHURT
450 g (1 lb/generous 1¾ cups) thick and creamy Turkish or Greek yoghurt
2–3 garlic cloves, crushed with salt and finely chopped
sea salt, to taste

First, make the dough. Sift the flour and salt into a wide bowl and make a well in the middle. Pour in the egg, water and olive oil, and use your hands to draw the flour into the liquid until you have a dough. On a flour-dusted work surface, knead the dough for about 3–4 minutes until smooth and elastic. Cover with cling film (plastic wrap) and leave to rest in the refrigerator for 30 minutes.

Meanwhile, make the filling. Heat the oil in a wide, heavy pan over a medium–high heat, add the onion and sauté for 10–12 minutes until softened and starting to char. Stir in the chopped parsley and combine well, then leave to cool.

Place the chickpeas in a large bowl and remove any loose outer skins. Mash with a potato masher (I like to go in with my hands, but if you find this labour intensive you can use a food processor too). Stir in the cooled sautéed onions, cumin and *pul biber*, and season well with salt and pepper to taste (this filling needs good seasoning). Knead the mixture with your hands for a couple of minutes to combine well.

Grease a 40 cm (16 in) round or square baking dish with olive oil (or use 2 smaller dishes). Preheat the oven to 180°C fan/200°C/400°F/gas 6.

Cut the dough into three balls. Working with one piece of dough at a time (cover the rest with cling film so they don't dry out), roll it out on a lightly floured surface to a sheet, 30 × 24 cm (12 × 10 in). Using a sharp knife, cut the dough into 6 cm (2½ in) squares. Place a heaped ½ tablespoon of the filling into the middle of each square and pinch the two parallel ends together to form a little boat to secure the filling (lightly flour your fingers if handling the dough becomes too sticky). Repeat with the rest of the dough and filling, and place the *mantı* boats in the prepared baking dish/es, stacking them next to one another in one layer.

Bake uncovered for about 18 minutes, until the *mantı* boats are lightly golden.

FOR THE GARLIC YOGHURT, beat the yoghurt with the garlic in a medium bowl and season with salt to taste. Cover and set aside to bring to room temperature.

Ocak ve Fırın Yemekleri

FOR THE SAUCE
1 tablespoon olive oil
1½ tablespoons double
  concentrated tomato
  paste
460 ml (16 fl oz/scant 2
  cups) water

FOR THE SPICED OIL
60 ml (2 fl oz/¼ cup)
  olive oil
1 teaspoon (or more)
  pul biber
1 teaspoon dried mint

While the *mantı* are baking, make the sauce. Heat the oil in a medium pan, stir in the tomato paste until well combined, then pour in the water and season with salt and pepper. Bring to the boil, then turn the heat off.

Pour the sauce around the baked *mantı* boats (it should reach a depth of about 5 mm/¼ in) and bake for a further 8–10 minutes until most of the sauce is absorbed. Take the baking dish out of the oven and keep it covered with foil.

FOR THE SPICED OIL, pour the olive oil into a small pan and stir in the *pul biber* and dried mint. Stir for 30–40 seconds over a low heat to infuse, then turn the heat off.

Arrange the *mantı* boats on a serving dish and spoon the garlic yoghurt over them, then drizzle with the spiced oil. Serve immediately.

Pazılı, Cevizli Erişte

Erişte Noodles with Chard, Walnuts and Crumbly Cheese

Serves 2–3

We use *erişte*, our traditional egg noodles, in a variety of ways (see also my comforting soup, *Erişteli Yesil Mercimek Çorbası*, on page 80). Here the pasta is combined with other vegetables for an easy, delicious dish. With crunchy walnuts, sweet pepper and slightly bitter chard, it makes a nourishing meal. You can use kale or other leafy greens as an alternative to chard. *Tulum peyniri*, our crumbly cheese made from sheeps' and goats' milk all over Anatolia, is lovely with *erişte*. You can use regular goats' cheese, *beyaz peynir* or feta as a substitute. My *erişte* recipe is on page 80, and it is satisfying to make your own. If pressed for time, you can use fresh tagliatelle instead.

2 tablespoons olive oil
1 red (bell) pepper, deseeded, quartered and thinly sliced
3 garlic cloves, finely chopped
150 g (5 oz) Swiss Chard, kale or other leafy greens, thinly sliced
sea salt and freshly ground black pepper, to taste
1 tablespoon lemon juice
60 ml (2 fl oz/¼ cup) water
30 g (1 oz/¼ cup) shelled walnuts, chopped
160 g (5½ oz) *Erişte* noodles (see page 80) (or fresh tagliatelle), cut into 6 cm (2½ in) strips
55 g (2 oz) *tulum*, *beyaz peynir*, feta or goats' cheese, crumbled
extra-virgin olive oil, for drizzling

Heat the olive oil in a wide sauté pan over a medium-high heat, add the peppers and sauté for 5 minutes, stirring often. Stir in the garlic and chard, season with salt and pepper, and sauté for 2–3 minutes (if using kale, give it a further 2 minutes). Add the lemon juice, water and walnuts, combine everything well for a couple of minutes, then remove from the heat.

Bring a pan of salted water to the boil, add the *erişte* and simmer for 8–10 minutes until the noodles are cooked but still have some bite (if using fresh tagliatelle, cook for 3–5 minutes or according to the package instructions). Drain and combine with the vegetable sauce over a gentle heat to warm through. Adjust the seasoning to your taste.

Serve immediately with cheese crumbled over and a drizzle of extra-virgin olive oil if you like.

+ **Prepare ahead:** You can make both *erişte* and the vegetable sauce ahead of time. Once completely dried, *erişte* can be stored in a clean muslin bag in a dry, cool, dark place for 1–2 months. Keep the vegetable sauce covered in the refrigerator for 1–2 days.

+ **Serving suggestion:** My zingy pickle, *Pancar ve Şalgam Turşusu* (page 216), complements this well.

Ocak ve Fırın Yemekleri

Fırında Patates Paçası

Turkish Garlicky Mashed Potatoes

Serves 6–8

Patates paçası is a popular specialty from the province of Kastamonu in the Black Sea region. It is a significant dish, too, as the EU granted PGI (protected geographical indication) status to the region's highly nutritious Taşköprü garlic, known as 'the white gold', which is used in this recipe by locals. These mashed potatoes are traditionally cooked on the stovetop with butter, yoghurt, eggs and garlic, and I love the lightness the yoghurt brings. I finish my version in the oven with grated cheese on top (*kaşar*, a medium-hard pale yellow cheese mostly made from sheeps' milk is the traditional choice, although you can use any melting cheese you have to hand). It is easy, humble, delicious and a pure comfort food with a touch of spice from the *pul biber* butter.

1 kg (2 lb 4 oz) white potatoes, peeled and cut into 2.5 cm (1 in) chunks
sea salt and freshly ground black pepper, to taste
3 medium eggs, beaten
230 g (8 oz/scant 1 cup) whole milk yoghurt
4 large garlic cloves, crushed with sea salt and finely chopped
85 g (3 oz) salted butter, cubed, **plus 1 tablespoon,** melted
125 g (4 oz) medium Cheddar, grated

FOR THE PUL BIBER BUTTER
2 tablespoons salted butter
1 teaspoon *pul biber* (use a little more if you like heat!)

Place the potatoes in a large pan with a pinch of salt and cover with plenty of hot water. Bring to the boil, partially cover and cook over a medium-low heat for about 20 minutes, or until the potatoes are fully cooked. Drain and transfer to a large mixing bowl. Leave to cool for 5 minutes, then mash the potatoes with a pinch of salt and freshly ground black pepper.

Preheat the oven to 180°C fan/200°C/400°F/gas 6.

Combine the eggs, yoghurt and garlic in a small bowl, mixing until well combined.

Melt the 85 g (3 oz) cubed butter in a large, wide pan over a medium heat, add the mashed potatoes and combine for 2 minutes. Pour the yoghurt mixture over the mashed potatoes and season with salt and pepper. Cook over a low heat, stirring, for 4–5 minutes until well blended and smooth (you want a hummus-like consistency).

Grease a 20 cm (8 in) square baking dish with the extra tablespoon of melted butter and spoon the mashed potato mixture evenly into the dish. Sprinkle the grated cheese over the top in an even layer and gently press. Bake for 35–40 minutes until the cheese is melted and the top is golden, then remove from the oven.

FOR THE *PUL BIBER* BUTTER, melt the butter in a small pan and stir in the *pul biber*. Combine for 35–40 seconds over a low heat to infuse.

Gently prick the top of the mashed potatoes and pour the *pul biber* butter over. Serve immediately while hot.

+ **Serving suggestion:** Serve with pickles, for instance *Salatalık Turşusu* (page 217), and *Nar Ekşili, Cevizli Pancar* (page 92) for a delicious meal.

Turşu, Salça ve Soslar

Ten

Pickles, Condiments and Sauces

Turşu, Salça ve Soslar

I love how pickles (*turşu*) enhance and complement the flavour of a dish – we serve them with *meze*, casseroles, grills (broils) and savoury pastries; they really do lift a meal. Pickling vegetables is an ancient tradition for Turks, with its origins in 14th-century Ottoman cuisine, where vegetables were pickled so that seasonal produce could be enjoyed out of season, too.

This ancient preservation technique has well and truly stood the test of time – we Turks love pickles and have them with almost every meal. The benefits of pickles are numerous, too – they are excellent for our digestive system, supporting our gut health and wellbeing. Along with popular pickles, you will also find lesser-known ones in this chapter, such as *Patlıcan Turşusu* (page 214) – not only delicious but so pretty to serve, too.

In this chapter, I will also cover how to make our flavour-packed condiments, pomegranate molasses and *biber salçası* (pepper paste), which are fantastic in marinades, dressings and dips, adding layers of flavour to a dish – a must in my kitchen. Last but not least, our *Beğendi*, a smoked aubergine and béchamel sauce (page 221), also deserves a special mention: its flavour combinations are iconic and I hope you become a fan like me.

Patlıcan Turşusu

Pickled Stuffed Aubergines

Makes 2 litres
(70 fl oz)

I first had pickled aubergines (eggplant) at the iconic Asrı Turşucu, a pickle shop in Cihangir, Istanbul – they have been making a large variety of pickles for over 100 years. Stuffed with shredded cabbage, garlic and peppers, it was a delight to look at and taste. Baby aubergines are traditionally used, although if you can't find them you can use a small, firm variety, cut in half widthways. You will need long stalks of parsley (long leafy celery stalks are also common to use) to wrap the aubergines. They are a delicious accompaniment to *meze*, salads, casseroles and savoury pastries.

680 g (1 lb 8 oz) small to medium aubergines (eggplant)
large bunch of flat-leaf parsley, with long stalks
1 red (bell) pepper, deseeded and cut into 3 cm (1 in) wedges
10 garlic cloves

FOR THE STUFFING
85 g (3 oz) white cabbage, very thinly sliced
1½ teaspoons natural rock salt
2 garlic cloves, finely chopped
⅓ green (bell) pepper, thinly sliced

FOR THE BRINE
100 ml (3½ fl oz/scant ½ cup) grape or cider vinegar
370 ml (13 fl oz/1½ cups) water
1 tablespoon natural rock salt
1 teaspoon sugar

You will need a 2 litre (70 fl oz) glass jar with a tight seal

First sterilise your glass jar (see page 217).

Cut off the green stalk of the aubergines and cut a deep split lengthways in each, without cutting through to the skin on the opposite side, and leaving 1 cm (½ in) uncut at either end. Unless using baby aubergines, cut each aubergine in half widthways. Bring a large pan of water to the boil and add the aubergines. Bring back to the boil, then reduce to a simmer for 15 minutes, submerging the aubergines into the water often. Remove the aubergines with a slotted spoon to a large bowl of cold water to cool, then drain and squeeze out any excess moisture and place on a large plate.

Place the parsley stalks into the same simmering water for 2–3 minutes until softened. Remove with a slotted spoon to a plate and set aside.

FOR THE STUFFING, place the sliced cabbage in a bowl and add the salt. Work the salt into the cabbage with your hands, squashing and squeezing for 2 minutes. Add the chopped garlic and pepper, and combine well.

To stuff the aubergines, place a couple of long, wilted parsley stalks on a chopping board and place an aubergine half over the middle part of the stalk. Gently open and fill the cavity with some of the stuffing mixture, trying not to overfill. Place a wedge of red pepper on top to cover the stuffing. Wrap the parsley stalk around the stuffed aubergine and tie into a secure parcel. Repeat this procedure for the remaining aubergines and stuffing.

Combine the brine ingredients in a jug, mixing well with a spoon to dissolve the salt and sugar.

Place half of the garlic cloves in the bottom of the prepared jar, then carefully put the stuffed aubergines lengthways into the jar. Top with the remaining garlic cloves and any leftover pepper wedges and parsley. Pour the brine into the jar and gently press, making sure the liquid covers the top of the vegetables. Tightly close and seal. Gently shake the jar to make sure the liquid reaches all corners and is distributed evenly. Place the jar on a plate in case the brine leaks and store in a cool, dark place for 4 weeks. Do not open the jar before this time, as this will spoil the pickling process, letting the air into the jar.

Once the jar is opened, store your pickles in the refrigerator, covered, for 2–3 months.

Pancar ve Şalgam Turşusu

Pickled Beetroot, Carrot and Turnip

Makes 850 ml
(30 fl oz)

This is one of my favourite pickles – I absolutely adore *Pancar ve Şalgam Turşusu*. The natural sweetness of beets is fantastic when pickled and their bright colours are a feast for the eye, too. In the south, the juice of pickled turnips (*şalgam suyu*) is also a popular street drink – I love the sour, tangy taste. These pickles not only taste great and complement many dishes, but also have beneficial probiotic properties, which makes them gut-friendly.

8 garlic cloves, peeled
**230 g (8 oz) beetroot
 (beets)**, peeled and roughly
 sliced
120 g (4 oz) carrots, peeled
 and roughly sliced
150 g (5 oz) turnip, peeled
 and roughly sliced
**340 ml (12 fl oz/1½ cups)
 water**
**50 ml (2 fl oz/3
 tablespoons) grape
 vinegar (or cider vinegar)**
**1 tablespoon natural rock
 salt**
small bunch of parsley,
 washed and patted dry

**You will need a 850 ml
 (30 fl oz) glass jar with a
 tight seal**

First sterilise your glass jar (see page 217).

Place half of the garlic cloves in the bottom of the prepared jar, then add the beet, carrot and turnip slices. Top with the remaining garlic cloves, gently pat down and pack them tightly and evenly.

Prepare the pickling solution by combining the water, vinegar and rock salt in a jug, stirring to fully dissolve. Pour the mixture into the jar, making sure the liquid covers the top of the vegetables. Place the parsley on top, then tightly close and seal. Gently shake the jar to make sure the liquid reaches all corners and is distributed evenly. Place the jar on a plate in case the brine leaks and store in a cool, dark place for 4 weeks. Do not open the jar before this time, as this will spoil the pickling process, letting the air into the jar.

Once the jar is opened, store your pickles in the refrigerator, covered, for up to 2 months.

+ **Serving suggestions:** I love this *turşu* with *Kumpir* (page 166). It is also a lovely side to egg dishes, such as Unscrambled *Menemen* (page 62).

Salatalık Turşusu

Pickled Cucumbers

Makes 850 ml
(30 fl oz)

We Turks have a long passion and love for pickles (*turşu*) dating back to the Ottoman period. Known also as *torshi*, derived from the Persian *torsh* (sour), pickled vegetables are much-loved in the Middle East and Balkans, as well as in *Türkiye* (Turkey). There are over 100 different varieties of *turşu* at home, and we have special *turşu* shops selling only pickles. From aubergine (eggplant) to cucumbers, tomatoes, peppers, beetroot (beets), cabbage, carrots or onions, we love pickling vegetables. We enjoy pickles as part of *meze*, to add to salads, with our savoury pastries, with grills (broils) as well as with casseroles and pilafs; they greatly enhance the flavour of every dish. Grape vinegar is traditionally used in making *turşu*, although you can use cider vinegar, too.

8 garlic cloves, peeled
485 g (1 lb 1 oz) firm, small cucumbers, washed, dried and roughly sliced
340 ml (12 fl oz/1½ cups) water
50 ml (2 fl oz/3 tablespoons) grape vinegar (or cider vinegar)
1 tablespoon natural rock salt
small bunch of flat-leaf parsley, washed and patted dry

You will need a 850 ml (30 fl oz) glass jar with a tight seal

First sterilise your glass jar. Wash your jar and the lid in hot soapy water, but do not dry them. Instead, leave them to stand upside down on a roasting tray while they're still wet. Pop the tray into a preheated oven at 160°C fan/180°C/350°F/gas 4 for about 15 minutes. To clean the rubber ring seal, remove the seal before washing the jar and place in a small saucepan. Cover with water and boil for 3 minutes to sterilise. Let cool.

Place half of the garlic cloves in the bottom of the prepared jar, then add the cucumber slices. Top with the remaining garlic cloves, gently pat down and pack them tightly and evenly.

Prepare the pickling solution by combining the water, vinegar and rock salt in a jug, stirring to fully dissolve. Pour the mixture into the jar, making sure the liquid covers the top of the cucumbers. Place the parsley on top, then tightly close and seal. Gently shake the jar to make sure the liquid reaches all corners and is distributed evenly. Place the jar on a plate in case the brine leaks and store in a cool, dark place for 3 weeks. Do not open the jar before this time, as this will spoil the pickling process, letting the air into the jar.

Once the jar is opened, store your pickles in the refrigerator, covered, for up to 2 months.

+ **Tips:** Use glass jars for pickling and sterilise before using. Only use natural rock salt and make sure your vegetables are firm (smaller varieties are better). Use one type of vegetable in the jar or group them with similar textures as their fermentation times can differ. The ideal temperature to keep the pickle jars is at 17–20°C (00–00°F), in a dark place.

+ **Serving suggestions:** Add *turşu* to salads, such as *Karışık Mevsim Salatası* (page 124), for added texture and flavour. I love pickles with savoury pastries, such as *Ispanaklı Gül Böreği* (page 38), as well as with pilafs (try *Sebzeli Bulgur Pilavı*, page 182, they complement each other deliciously) and as part of a *meze* spread.

Biber Salçası

Homemade Turkish Red Pepper Paste

Makes 285 g
(10 oz)

GF V

I absolutely adore our flavour-packed, vibrant condiment, *biber salçası*, and liberally use it in sauces, dips, marinades, casseroles and soups – it instantly adds a depth of flavour and richness to our meals. Turkish red pepper paste is a fundamental ingredient in southern Turkish cuisine. In my hometown of Antakya, village women cook huge batches of freshly picked spicy and mild red peppers and spread them out on top of their cloth-covered terraces to dry under the hot summer sun until the peppers dehydrate and turn into this robust, flavour-packed condiment. I am unable to sun-dry my peppers where I live, so I make my own version of red pepper paste at home, cooking them on the stove top. It takes a bit of time to make but really is worth it.

6 firm red (bell) peppers, deseeded and cut into 4 cm (1½ in) chunks
370 ml (13 fl oz/1½ cups) hot water
3 small red chilli peppers, deseeded and finely chopped (use a few more if you like it spicier)
1½ teaspoons sea salt
1 tablespoon olive oil

You will need a 315 ml (11 oz) glass jar with a tight seal

First sterilise your glass jar (see page 217).

Place the chopped red (bell) peppers in a wide, heavy pan and add the hot water. Cook over a medium heat, stirring often, for 25 minutes – gently pressing and turning as you stir, they will start to break apart and soften and most of the liquid will be absorbed. Add the chilli peppers and keep on stirring and cooking over a low–medium heat for another 10 minutes. By the end of this time the peppers will be cooked and the moisture evaporated. Leave to cool for 5 minutes.

Place the cooked peppers in a food processor and process until the mixture is almost a smooth purée (I like a little texture). Return the puréed peppers to the pan, season with the salt and cook over a low heat for a further 30–35 minutes, stirring continuously so the purée doesn't burn, until the juices have evaporated. The purée will shrink by half and turn into a soft paste. Remove from the heat.

Pour the paste into the prepared glass jar while still warm, and gently push down and shake a little to settle. Top with the olive oil and seal. When cool, keep your prepared paste in the refrigerator and use within 2–3 weeks.

+ **Serving suggestions:** Enjoy *Biber Salçası* with *Muhammara* (page 97), *Ezo Gelin Çorbası* (page 83) or to enhance the flavour of any dish.

Nar Ekşisi

Homemade Pomegranate Molasses

Makes 180 ml
(6 fl oz/⅞ cup)

Rich, tangy pomegranate molasses (*nar ekşisi*) is an essential condiment in southern Turkish cuisine. I have fond memories of watching my grandmother making her own pomegranate molasses at her home in Antakya, with wafting aromas of simmering pomegranate juice around her courtyard. This concentrated, fragrant molasses adds an exquisite flavour to salads, casseroles and dips. It is quite an effort to make homemade pomegranate molasses but its natural, fragrant taste is rewarding.

8–10 large pomegranates (to obtain 1 litre/34 fl oz/4 cups juice)
30 g (1 oz/2 tablespoons) brown sugar
1 tablespoon lemon juice

Remove all the pomegranate seeds from the fruit and place in a sieve set over a bowl. Place in the sink (to minimise mess) and squeeze the pomegranate seeds with your hands to extract as much juice as possible. Discard the leftover seeds.

Measure out 1 litre (34 fl oz/4 cups) of the freshly squeezed pomegranate juice into a heavy saucepan. Stir in the sugar and bring to the boil over a medium–high heat, stirring until the sugar is dissolved. Mix in the lemon

juice and reduce the heat to medium-low, just enough for simmering. Simmer for about 65–70 minutes, stirring every 10 minutes; the juice will thicken and reduce in volume.

Turn the heat off and let the pomegranate molasses cool. It will thicken more as it cools.

Once cool, store in a sterilised (see page 217), airtight glass jar. The molasses will keep in the refrigerator for up to 1 month.

Beğendi

Smoked Aubergine and Béchamel Sauce

Serves 4 generously

Creamy, smoked aubergine (eggplant) flesh combined with béchamel sauce is traditionally served with lamb cubes cooked in tomato sauce, as in the iconic Hünkar Beğendi, a much-loved classic from the Ottoman palace kitchens. I love *Beğendi* sauce so much that I can literally eat it on its own with a spoon. It is a versatile sauce and equally delicious, though not traditional, over roasted vegetables – meaty aubergines, mushrooms or squash make brilliant accompaniments. To get the smoky flavour, cook the aubergines directly over a burner, open gas flame or on a barbecue grill.

3 medium aubergines
  (eggplant)
juice of ½ small lemon
55 g (2 oz) butter
85 g (3 oz/⅔ cup) plain
  (all-purpose) flour
  (use gluten-free flour if
  preferred)
500 ml (17 fl oz/2 cups)
  whole milk, warmed
sea salt and freshly ground
  black pepper, to taste
120 g (4 oz) medium
  Cheddar cheese, grated

Cook the aubergines on a barbecue grill or over an open gas flame, turning every 2–3 minutes with metal tongs, until the outer skin is charred and blistered and the inner flesh soft. Depending on the size of the aubergines, they should be ready in about 25 minutes. Alternatively, if you prefer not to have the smoky flavour, you can prick the aubergines in 4–5 places and bake in a 200°C fan/220°C/425°F/gas 7 oven for about 40 minutes, or until they feel very soft when pressed and the skins are wrinkled (turn them over halfway through cooking). When cool enough to handle, peel away the burnt skins and discard the stalks.

Put the aubergine flesh in a colander to drain away any bitter juices and gently squeeze. Chop coarsely and mash in a bowl with the lemon juice using a fork.

Make the béchamel sauce by melting the butter in a medium pan over a low-medium heat. Add the flour and beat well to make a white sauce. Slowly add the warm milk, whisking continuously to get a smooth consistency, and cook for about 3–4 minutes until the sauce is thickened. Add the mashed aubergines with a little salt and pepper, and simmer for a further 2 minutes. Stir in the cheese and combine for a minute, then remove from the heat and serve.

+ **Prepare ahead:** You can prepare the smoked aubergine flesh ahead of time and keep covered in the refrigerator.

+ **Serving suggestions:** Serve *Beğendi* sauce over *Fırında Sebzeli, Nohutlu Türlü* (page 194) or with *Turkish Şakşuka* (page 108). To reheat the sauce, add 1 tablespoon of milk and warm over a gentle heat for 2–3 minutes, stirring continuously.

Kek, Kurabiye, Tatlılar

Eleven

Sweets

Kek, Kurabiye, Tatlılar

In Turkish culture, sweets are the centrepiece at religious festivals, weddings and family celebrations. We have a variety of sweet treats – they can be milk-, fruit- or grain-based, or made with *yufka* (filo) sheets; there's something for everyone. This chapter offers delightful Turkish classics, such as the creamy *Şöbiyet* filo triangles (page 234), which will melt in your mouth and you will be pleasantly surprised how easy they are to make. *Balkabaklı, Cevizli Havuç Dilimi Baklava* (pumpkin and walnut baklava, page 226), my creation, may become your go-to dessert for festive times. I am especially partial to our fruit-based desserts and I would love you to try *Kuru Kayısı Tatlısı* (page 231), deliciously fragrant and so easy to make. This chapter also includes showstopper cakes, such as the citrussy *Portakallı Revani* (page 232), along with delightful *kurabiyes* (cookies). I do hope you have a go at my favourite bitter almond cookies, *Acıbadem Kurabiyesi* (page 238), their chewy texture is so satisfying – the perfect treat with tea or coffee.

Balkabaklı, Cevizli Havuç Dilimi Baklava

Pumpkin and Walnut Baklava

Serves 12

The Turkish love pumpkin in desserts (either baked in its own juice with sugar or poached in syrup) and baklava are a legacy of the Ottoman palace kitchens. Baked in a round tray and sliced into wedges, *havuç dilimi* is one of our traditional baklava shapes and traditionally walnuts and/or pistachios are used in the filling and as decoration. Here, I combined luscious pumpkin with crunchy walnuts and warming cinnamon to make a delicious seasonal filling for my baklava. It is an impressive (and lighter) version of baklava to serve, especially during the festive season.

150 g (5 oz) **unsalted butter,** melted (or plant-based alternative or vegetable oil)

21 thin **filo sheets (or *baklavalık yufka),*** thawed

1 tablespoon **crushed walnuts or pistachios,** to decorate

Turkish thick cream (*kaymak*) or clotted cream (or plant-based alternative), to serve

FOR THE SYRUP

340 g (12 oz/generous 1½ cups) **granulated sugar**

300 ml (10 fl oz/1¼ cups) **water**

6 **cloves**

juice of **½ small lemon**

FOR THE FILLING

700 g (1 lb 9 oz) **pumpkin or butternut squash,** peeled, deseeded and cut into 2 cm (¾ in) chunks (prepared weight)

2 tablespoons **granulated sugar**

125 g (4 oz/1 cup) **shelled walnuts,** finely chopped

1 tablespoon **ground cinnamon**

First, prepare the syrup. Put the sugar into a medium, heavy pan, pour in the water and bring to the boil, stirring all the time. When the sugar is dissolved, reduce the heat and stir in the cloves and the lemon juice. Simmer for about 25 minutes until the syrup starts to thicken slightly, coating the back of the spoon. Remove the cloves and leave to cool in the pan.

Preheat the oven to 180°C fan/200°C/400°F/gas 6. Line a large baking sheet with baking paper.

TO MAKE THE FILLING, place the pumpkin or butternut squash slices on the baking sheet in one layer. Sprinkle over the sugar and bake for 35 minutes until softened. Leave to cool, then finely chop the pumpkin or butternut into pieces the size of pine nuts and place in a bowl. Stir in the chopped walnuts and cinnamon, and gently combine well.

Turn the oven temperature down to 160°C fan/180°C/350°F/gas 4.

Melt the butter over a gentle heat in a small pan and skim off the white foam that forms on top. Brush the base and sides of a 25 cm (10 in) baking dish (round or square) with the melted butter.

Take the filo sheets out of the package and cut into discs or squares to fit into your baking dish. Place them on a clean, dry surface and cover with a damp towel. Place a filo sheet over the buttered baking dish and brush with more melted butter. Continue in this way until you have used 12 filo sheets. Gently spoon the filling mixture on top, leaving 1 cm (½ in) around the edges filling free. Gently pat down so that the filling is intact and smooth in one layer. Place another filo sheet on top and brush with melted butter, then continue in this way until you have used up all the pastry. Tuck the edges in to seal with the buttered brush. Use a sharp knife to slice through all the layers and cut into quarters, then cut each quarter into three wedges.

Gently butter the top layer of pastry again and bake for 55–60 minutes, or until the top is golden. Take the baklava out of the oven and pour the cooled syrup over the hot baklava. Return the baklava to the oven for another 8–10 minutes, then remove and leave to cool.

Once cool, sprinkle the crushed nuts in the middle of the baklava. Gently remove slices to serving plates and serve with a dollop of *kaymak* or clotted cream (or plant-based alternative) on the side.

Kek, Kurabiye, Tatlılar

✦ **Prepare ahead:** You can prepare the filling and the syrup a day ahead, cover and keep at room temperature. You can also prepare the whole baklava ahead of time – they will keep well for 3–4 days, covered, at room temperature.

✦ **Tip:** Thin filo pastry sheets or *baklavalık yufka* works best for making baklava. Leftover filo sheets can be wrapped in cling film (plastic wrap) and kept in the refrigerator for a few days. You can use them to make *Otlu Tava Böreği* (page 40).

Ayva Tatlısı

Poached Quince Dessert

Serves 4

The fragrant *Ayva tatlısı* is a popular winter dessert at home, served with our thick cream (*kaymak*). Quince is gently poached in sugar, cloves and cinnamon, along with its peel and seeds. The seeds contain pectin, a natural thickener, so please do make sure to use them. Slow, gentle cooking is the key here, which transforms the hard and tart quince into a soft, delicate, ruby-coloured dessert. The cooked peels are a bonus delight, and another good example of the no-waste Turkish kitchen – you can chop and enjoy them over toast or mixed with yoghurt and nuts for breakfast.

2 medium quinces
  (620 g/1 lb 6 oz)
3 tablespoons lemon juice
170 g (6 oz/¾ cup)
  granulated sugar
370 ml (12½ fl oz/1½ cups)
  water
10 cloves
1 tablespoon ground
  cinnamon
Turkish thick cream
  (*kaymak*), clotted cream
  or plant-based cream, to
  serve
1 tablespoon finely
  chopped pistachios or
  walnuts, to serve

Wash and cut the quinces in half lengthways. Scoop out the core and remove the seeds, then set the seeds aside. Peel the skin of the quince halves and save the peels, too. Rub the peeled quince halves with the lemon juice to prevent it discolouring.

Spread the quince peels in a heavy pan, wide enough to have 4 quince halves in one layer. Place the quince halves, hollow sides up, side by side over the peels. Sprinkle the sugar evenly over the quinces, then pour in the water and stir in the reserved quince seeds and cloves. Bring to the boil, then reduce the heat to low, cover and simmer gently for about 45 minutes.

After this time, check the quinces and flip the halves gently over. The quinces will start turning a rosy, darkish pink colour and the syrup will start to thicken. Stir in the ground cinnamon, cover and cook over a low heat for a further 1 hour, basting the quinces with the juices every 20 minutes or so (you may need a little more or less cooking time depending on the size of the quinces) until slightly caramelised. Leave to cool in the pan. While it sits, the syrup will thicken even more and the colour will go darker.

Once cool, place the quince halves on a serving plate, and serve with a dollop of clotted cream or Turkish *kaymak* and a sprinkle of crushed pistachios or walnuts.

+ **Prepare ahead:** You can prepare this dessert in advance; it keeps well in the refrigerator, covered, for 2–3 days.

Kuru Kayısı Tatlısı

Poached Dried Apricots in Light Syrup with Clotted Cream

Serves 8–10

(GF) (VO)

This is a light, delicious and easy dessert for entertaining. *Türkiye* (Turkey) is one of the largest producers of apricots (*kayısı*). They are grown in abundance during the summer months, and some of the yearly harvest is dried in the sun to be enjoyed all year round. Malatya, a city in the southeast, is particularly famous for the quality of its dried apricots, which are exported all over the world. When I was a child, we lived in Elazığ, a city next to Malatya, and my father would bring home cases of juicy apricots after work. We would eagerly wait for my father's return and the apricots would soon disappear. Poaching dried apricots in light syrup brings out their beautiful fragrance and they are luscious served with cream.

150 g (5 oz/⅔ cup) granulated sugar
450 ml (15 fl oz/1¾ cups) hot water
1 tablespoon fresh lemon juice
250 g (9 oz) soft dried apricots
85 g (3 oz/⅓ cup) Turkish thick cream *(kaymak)* or clotted cream (or plant-based clotted cream)
2 tablespoons crushed pistachios

Combine the sugar and hot water in a medium pan and bring to the boil. Stir constantly until the sugar dissolves, then reduce to a simmer. Pour in the lemon juice and add the dried apricots, and poach for 20 minutes over a low–medium heat. The apricots will plump up and the syrup will thicken, infused with the apricots' beautiful fragrance. Leave to cool.

Once cool, gently open the split of the apricot and fill each with about ⅓ teaspoon *kaymak* or clotted cream. Place the stuffed apricots on a serving dish, spoon the syrup around them and sprinkle with crushed pistachios to serve.

+ **Prepare ahead:** You can poach the dried apricots in syrup 1–2 days ahead. Once cool, keep in a container, covered, in the refrigerator.

+ **Variation and leftovers:** Instead of clotted cream, you can stuff the dried apricots with 85 g (3 oz/⅔ cup) chopped walnuts for a plant-based feast. Leftovers can be enjoyed for breakfast or you can serve the leftover syrup as a light sherbet drink, with ice cubes and fresh mint in small glasses.

Portakallı Revani

Semolina Sponge Cake with Orange Slices

Serves 6-8

Revani is a lovely, moist semolina sponge cake in light syrup, and one of the most popular desserts at home; variations are enjoyed throughout the Eastern Mediterranean, too. I love the grainy texture of semolina and the lightness it gives to the cake. There are many versions of *revani*; when made with orange, often the zest and in some cases the juice is used. In my version I used thinly sliced oranges as well as fresh orange juice in the syrup. The glazed orange slices on top look so pretty and add a deliciously citrussy, fragrant taste.

60 ml (2 fl oz/¼ cup) **light olive oil**, plus extra for greasing
3 medium **eggs**
170 g (6 oz/¾ cup) **granulated sugar**
225 g (8 oz/scant 1 cup) **plain whole milk yoghurt**
170 g (6 oz/⅞ cup) **coarse semolina**
40 g (1½ oz/⅓ cup) **plain (all-purpose) flour**
1 teaspoon **baking powder**
1 tablespoon **ground pistachios or desiccated (dried shredded) coconut**, to decorate
Turkish thick cream (*kaymak*) or clotted cream, to serve (optional)

FOR THE ORANGES IN SYRUP

100 ml (3½ fl oz) **freshly squeezed orange juice**
300 g (10½ oz/1⅓ cups) **granulated sugar**
280 ml (9½ fl oz/scant 1¼ cups) **water**
1 medium **orange, thinly sliced into 3 mm (⅛ in) discs**
1 tablespoon **lemon juice**

Make the oranges in syrup first. Pour the freshly squeezed orange juice through a sieve to get rid of the pulp. Combine the sugar, orange juice and water in a large pan and stir over a medium heat until the sugar is dissolved, then add the orange slices and lemon juice. Simmer gently for 25–30 minutes until the orange slices soften. Remove from the heat and use a slotted spoon to gently remove the orange slices to a plate. Cut each slice in half and arrange them side by side. Reserve the syrup and set aside to cool.

Preheat the oven to 180°C fan/200°C/400°F/gas 6. Grease a 20 cm (8 in) round cake pan or baking dish with a little light olive oil and line with baking paper.

Beat the eggs and combine with the sugar in a large mixing bowl for a few minutes until the sugar dissolves. Add the light olive oil, yoghurt, semolina, flour and baking powder, and combine well until you have a smooth batter.

Arrange the sliced oranges side by side in the prepared cake pan. Gently pour the batter over the top and bake for 30–32 minutes until the top of the cake is golden brown and an inserted skewer comes out clean.

Using a large spoon, drizzle the cooled syrup all over the hot semolina cake. Let the cake absorb the syrup and cool down for 15 minutes in the pan, then carefully turn the cake out onto a large flat serving plate. Gently remove the baking paper to reveal the glossy top with glazed orange slices. Sprinkle over the ground pistachios or desiccated coconut to decorate.

Slice and enjoy warm or at room temperature. Turkish *kaymak* or clotted cream is lovely on the side, if you like. This cake keeps well for 2–3 days in an airtight container in a cool place.

+ **Prepare ahead:** You can make the syrup with orange slices a day ahead and keep covered at room temperature. Please use freshly squeezed orange juice in the syrup, as it does make a difference.

Şöbiyet

Baklava Triangles with Semolina Cream and Pistachio

Makes 12

This delightful treat hails from the Gaziantep region, famous for its baklava. Creamy and soft on the inside, with crunchy, syrupy filo on the outside, they are especially enjoyed at religious festivities as well as on special occasions. Locals may add *kaymak* (Turkish thick clotted cream made from water buffalo milk) to the filling and some make this semolina cream. I find making the filling with single (light) cream gives the best result. Thin filo sheets or *baklavalık yufka* also work best here. Enjoy with tea or coffee, as we do at home.

125 g (4 oz) unsalted butter
10 thin filo pastry sheets (*baklavalık yufka*), thawed (each sheet 35 × 30 cm/ 14 × 12 in)
15 g (½ oz/1½ tablespoons) pistachios, very finely chopped, to fill, plus 1 tablespoon finely chopped pistachios, to decorate

FOR THE SYRUP
300 g (10½ oz/1⅓ cups) granulated sugar
285 ml (9½ fl oz/generous 1 cup) water
juice of ½ small lemon (about 1 tablespoon)

FOR THE SEMOLINA CREAM
40 g (1½ oz/⅓ cup) fine semolina
285 ml (9½ fl oz/generous 1 cup) single (light) cream

First, prepare the syrup. Put the sugar into a medium heavy pan, pour in the water and bring to the boil, stirring all the time. When the sugar is dissolved, reduce the heat and stir in the lemon juice. Simmer for 20–25 minutes until the syrup starts to thicken slightly, coating the back of the spoon. Leave to cool in the pan.

FOR THE SEMOLINA CREAM, combine the semolina and cream in a small pan and set over a medium heat, stirring continuously. When it starts bubbling, reduce the heat to low and cook for 3–4 minutes, stirring continuously. The semolina will absorb all the liquid and it will thicken, sliding off the spoon as lumps. Turn the heat off, place the semolina cream in a small bowl and set aside to cool (it will thicken further as it sits).

Melt the butter over a low heat in a small pan and skim off the white froth that forms. Brush a 25 cm (10 in) round or square baking dish with the melted butter. Preheat the oven to 160°C fan/180°C/350°F/gas 4.

Place the thawed filo sheets on a clean, dry surface and cover with a damp towel. Brush each filo sheet with the melted butter and carefully stack on top of one another. Do not brush the top of the last sheet. Use a sharp knife to cut the sheets through all the layers into 12 rough squares (each about 10 × 8.5 cm/4 x 3½ in). Place a generously heaped tablespoon of semolina cream in the middle of each filo square and top with a little less than ½ teaspoon of very finely chopped pistachios. Fold each block of buttered, stacked filo square over the filling to form a triangle. Gently pinch the ends with your fingers to close and seal each triangle.

Place the filo triangles on the greased baking dish, stacking the corner of each triangle slightly under another so that they won't open during baking. Brush the tops and sides of each triangle with the melted butter.

Bake for 55–60 minutes until golden on top. Remove from the oven and cool slightly for 3 minutes, then pour the cooled syrup over and leave to soak for 15–20 minutes, gently pouring the syrup from the baking dish over the *Şöbiyet* a few times. Sprinkle a few finely chopped pistachios over the corner of each *Şöbiyet* and serve at room temperature.

Fırın Sütlaç

Baked Turkish Rice Pudding

Serves 6

One of the most popular milk-based puddings, the origins of *Fırın Sütlaç* date back to Ottoman cuisine. It is enjoyed all through the country with variations, during festivities and as an everyday treat, and can be found in *pastane* (patisseries) and *muhallebici* (pudding shops). I have fond memories of stopping by our local *muhallebici* in Istanbul to enjoy *Fırın Sütlaç* with a glass of çay after school with friends as a treat – and now my children love it, too.

Chopped nuts, such as pistachios, and hazelnuts in the Black Sea region, can be added over the top as decoration. Rice flour can be used instead of cornflour (cornstarch) to thicken the pudding and some versions include egg yolk. I suggest using whole milk if you can, for the creamy taste and texture. It is traditionally enjoyed cold, although I equally love it warm or at room temperature.

125 g (4 oz/generous ½ cup) short-grain pudding rice, rinsed

450 ml (15 fl oz/1¾ cups) whole milk (for stage 1)

1 litre (34 fl oz/4 cups) whole milk (for stage 2)

1 teaspoon vanilla extract

160 g (5 ½ oz) granulated sugar

3 tablespoons cornflour (cornstarch)

85 ml (3 fl oz) whole milk (for stage 3)

1½ tablespoons finely chopped pistachios and/ or hazelnuts, to decorate

Combine the rice with the milk for stage 1 in a large heavy saucepan, stir and bring to the boil over a medium heat. Once it starts bubbling, reduce the heat to low, cover and simmer for about 20 minutes until all the milk is absorbed. Make sure to check and stir occasionally so the rice doesn't stick to the bottom of the pan, especially towards the end.

Now add the stage 2 milk to the cooked rice, stir and bring to the boil, then reduce to a simmer. Stir in the vanilla extract and sugar.

In a small bowl, whisk the cornflour with the stage 3 milk to a smooth paste and add this to the rice mixture. Simmer over a low–medium heat, stirring constantly, for about 20 minutes.

Meanwhile, preheat the oven to 200°C fan/220°C/425°F/gas 7.

By now, the pudding will have thickened but should still be pourable. Turn the heat off (the pudding will thicken further as it sits). Pour the pudding into six 9 cm (3½ in) ovenproof ramekins, making sure to leave 2 cm (¾ in) at the top of the pots unfilled as the pudding tends to rise while baking. Place the ramekins in a large roasting tin and pour in enough water to come halfway up the sides of the ramekins.

Bake for 20–25 minutes, or until the pudding tops are nicely patched with brown. Please keep an eye on them towards the end so that the puddings don't over brown. Carefully remove from the tin and leave to cool for 10 minutes.

I love to serve this warm, decorated with nuts. If you prefer the traditional way, cool to room temperature, then cover and refrigerate for 2–3 hours. Sprinkle with nuts and serve cold.

+ **Prepare ahead:** As *Fırın Sütlaç* is traditionally served cold, you can make it a day ahead and keep covered in the refrigerator.

Türk Kahveli Mermer Kek

Turkish Coffee Marble Cake

Serves 8–10

Turkish coffee (*Türk kahvesi*) is my favourite hot drink and it really is more than a drink for us with its proud history, traditions and rituals. It is made from 100 per cent Arabica beans that have to be toasted to the roasting point and ground to a very fine powder. I have fond memories of enjoying Turkish coffee with my mum, Gülçin – it was a precious moment for us to pause and enjoy this special drink in good company. Turkish coffee is not only enjoyed as a drink at home, but it also appears in sweet bakes, such as this marble cake. This is a deliciously moist and fragrant, but not overpowering, coffee cake.

175 g (6 oz) **unsalted butter,** plus extra for greasing

2 tablespoons **Turkish coffee** (finely ground)

90 ml (3 fl oz/6 tablespoons) **warm whole milk**

1 tablespoon **cocoa powder**

225 g (8 oz/1 cup) **granulated sugar**

3 medium **eggs,** beaten

½ teaspoon **vanilla extract**

230 g (8 oz/generous 1¾ cups) **self-raising flour,** sifted

pinch of salt

2 tablespoons **cold whole milk**

Preheat the oven to 160°C fan/180°C/350°F/gas 4. Grease a 2 lb loaf pan or 20 cm (8 in) round cake pan (or non-stick fluted cake ring) with unsalted butter.

Combine the Turkish coffee with the warm milk and stir until completely dissolved. Stir in the cocoa powder and set aside to cool.

Using an electric whisk, cream the butter and sugar in a large mixing bowl until pale and fluffy. Add the beaten eggs a little at a time, whisking well after each addition, then stir in the vanilla extract and combine well. Sift the flour and salt into a separate bowl, then fold it gently but thoroughly into the butter mixture.

Divide the cake batter into two equal portions. Add the 2 tablespoons of cold milk to one portion of the cake batter and stir gently to combine. Stir the cooled Turkish coffee mixture into the other portion of cake batter and stir gently to combine.

Spoon large blobs of each cake batter into the prepared cake pan, alternating the flavours. Swirl the batter gently with a skewer or chopstick to create a marbled effect. Bake for 42–45 minutes until the cake is springy and an inserted skewer comes out clean. Allow the cake to cool in the tin for 10 minutes, then turn out onto a serving plate to cool completely before slicing.

This cake will keep well for up to 3 days in a container, covered.

Acıbadem Kurabiyesi

Bitter Almond Cookies

Makes 10

I absolutely adore crispy on the outside, chewy on the inside *Acıbadem Kurabiyesi*. Their origins date back to 19th-century Ottoman palace kitchens and the traditional recipe includes a small amount of bitter almonds, hence the name. Our world-famous almonds from the Datça region are traditionally used in these cookies. They have a macaron-like chewy texture. Living abroad, it is one of those tastes I miss so much from home and I think many Turks living abroad would feel the same. The good news is that you can make these delicious almond cookies at home easily and successfully in no time. They are absolutely delightful with Turkish coffee or tea.

3 medium egg whites
 (100 g/3½ oz)
200 g (7 oz/scant 1 cup)
 granulated sugar
pinch of sea salt
½ teaspoon lemon juice
180 g (6½ oz/1¾ cups)
 ground almonds
10 unsalted almonds

Preheat the oven to 140°C fan/160°C/325°F/gas 3.

Half-fill a large pan with hot water and sit a heatproof mixing bowl over the pan. Make sure the bowl is not touching the water. Bring to a gentle simmer and combine the egg whites, sugar, salt and lemon juice in the bowl. Stir continuously to combine over a simmering heat for about 4–5 minutes until the sugar is melted completely. The mixture should be warm enough to touch (around 65°C/150°F if using a sugar thermometer) and have a gooey texture. Remove from the heat.

Stir the ground almonds into the sugar mixture and combine well until you have a very soft, sticky dough. Leave to cool, stirring occasionally until completely cold, then spoon the mixture into a piping bag.

Line a large baking sheet with a piece of baking paper, sticking down the corners with a little of the remaining cookie mixture from the bowl. Pipe about ten 6 cm (2½ in) circles of cookie

mixture over the baking paper, leaving 3 cm (1 in) between each cookie as they will expand during baking. Place an almond in the middle of each cookie.

Bake for 27–29 minutes until the cookies look cracked and crispy on the outside but are still soft on the inside (it is important not to overbake and keep the inside soft, as this moisture will help the cookies stick together, as is traditional, and will give the chewy texture).

Place the baking sheet on a metal rack to cool for 10 minutes. If the cookies are sticking to the baking paper, gently turn the baking paper upside down on the baking sheet and wipe the back of the cookies over the baking paper with a damp towel – this will help the cookies peel away from the paper easily. Place the *acıbadem kurabiyesi* on a serving plate. If you like, gently press the soft bottoms of two cookies together to form one big cookie, as we traditionally do, or leave as individual cookies. They are best eaten on the day, although they keep well for 2–3 days, wrapped individually in cling film (plastic wrap) and stored in a cool place.

Fıstıklı Un Kurabiyesi

Turkish Shortbread Cookies with Pistachio

Makes 25

These delicious, crumbly shortbread cookies are a national favourite. My mother would make them for her afternoon tea gatherings and special occasions when I was a child and now my children adore these, too. You will find them in Turkish *pastanes* (patisseries) either plain, or with nuts or dried fruits. They are delicious enjoyed with Turkish coffee (*Türk kahvesi*) and tea (*çay*). I add coarsely ground pistachios to mine for a fragrant nutty taste. Turkish pistachios (*fıstık*) are regarded as our green emeralds and are packed with flavour.

90 g (3¼ oz/scant ⅔ cup) shelled unsalted pistachios, plus a little extra to serve

300 g (10½ oz/scant 2½ cups) plain (all-purpose) flour

125 g (4 oz/1 cup) icing (confectioners') sugar, plus extra for dusting

250 g (9 oz) unsalted butter, cubed

½ teaspoon baking powder

pinch of sea salt

1 teaspoon vanilla extract

Coarsely chop or grind the pistachios with a few pulses in a food processor; take care not to grind too finely, as it's lovely to retain a little texture.

Sift the flour into a large bowl and set aside. Sift the icing sugar into a separate bowl.

Put the butter in a large mixing bowl. Beat using a hand-held electric mixer for 2 minutes until smooth and light. Stir in the icing sugar and beat for another 2 minutes until well combined. Add the sifted flour, baking powder, salt and vanilla extract, and beat for another 2 minutes, making sure everything is combined well. Stir in the pistachios and beat for another minute or two until all combined and turned into a crumbly dough. Using your hands, gently form into a dough ball, place in a bowl, cover with cling film (plastic wrap) and chill in the refrigerator for 15 minutes.

Preheat the oven to 160°C fan/180°C/350°F/gas 4. Line a large baking sheet with baking paper.

Take the dough out of the refrigerator and gently shape walnut-sized pieces of dough into round balls with your hands. Each dough ball will be about 3.5 cm (1½ in) in diameter. Place on the baking sheet, with about 5 cm (2 in) between each ball, as they will expand. You should be able to make 25 balls.

Bake on the lower shelf of the oven for 18–20 minutes until the cookies are pale golden; try not to overbake, so that they can retain their crumbly texture and light colour. Remove from the oven and let cool completely.

Once cool, sift over some icing sugar and sprinkle with a little ground pistachio to serve.

✢ **Prepare ahead:** These will keep well in an airtight container for 4 days.

Kuru İncir Reçeli

Dried Fig Jam

Makes 385 g
(13½ oz)

(GF) (V)

I absolutely adore figs – we enjoy them fresh as well as dried. *Türkiye* (Turkey) is a large fig producer (75 per cent of dried fig exports are Turkish) and they grow mainly in the Aegean, in the Mediterranean, southeast Anatolian and Marmara regions. Growing up in ancient Antioch, Antakya, picking up fresh, ripe figs from the tree in my grandmother's courtyard was one of my favourite things to do; they always smelled so fragrant, with a juicy, heavenly taste. Excess produce would be dried to be enjoyed out of season. This dried fig jam is one of the delicious ways to enjoy this fascinating fruit and it is so easy to make.

250 g (9 oz) soft dried figs, stalk removed, finely diced
170 ml (6 fl oz/¾ cup) water
80 g (3 oz/⅓ cup) granulated sugar
zest of 1 small lemon, plus 1 tablespoon fresh lemon juice
1 teaspoon ground cinnamon

You will need a 400 ml (14 fl oz) glass jar with a tight seal

Place the chopped dried figs, water and sugar in a medium saucepan over a medium heat and cook, stirring constantly, until the sugar is dissolved and it starts bubbling. Reduce the heat and simmer for 10 minutes, stirring often, then add the lemon zest and juice, and cinnamon, and simmer for another 8 minutes, stirring often. At the end of this time, the mixture will thicken and the figs will be soft and jammy. Remove from the heat and leave the fig jam to cool in the pan.

Once cool, spoon the jam into a sterilised jar (see page 217) and seal. Store in a cool, dry place for up to 3 months.

+ **Note:** If the dried figs are quite hard, you can soak them in a bowl of hot water for 2 minutes to soften, then drain and chop, ready for cooking.

+ **Serving suggestions:** This dried fig jam is lovely over fresh bread or *Simit* (page 168). I also love it with *Kaygana* crêpes (page 58).

Menu Suggestions

Turkish Brunch

— *Simit*, **Sesame-Encrusted Turkish Bread Rings** (page 168)
— *Çılbır*, **Turkish-Style Poached Eggs in Garlicky Yoghurt** (page 61)
— *Kaygana*, **Crêpes with Parsley and Spring Onions** (page 58)
— *Nar Ekşili Zeytin Salatası*, **Olive Salad with Pomegranate Molasses and Walnuts** (page 66)
— *Kuru İncir Reçeli*, **Dried Fig Jam** (page 242)

Meze Feast

— *Balon Ekmek*, **Easy Puffy Bread** (page 44)
— *Nar Ekşili, Cevizli Pancar*, **Beetroot with Walnuts and Pomegranate Molasses** (page 92)
— *Öcce*, **Spring Onion Fritters with Fresh Herbs** (page 110)
— *Muhammara / Cevizli Biber*, **Walnut and Red Pepper Paste Dip** (page 97)
— *Cevizli, Yoğurtlu, Sarımsaklı Havuç ve Kabak*, **Garlicky Courgettes and Carrots with Walnuts in Yoghurt** (page 102)
— *Patlıcanlı Rulo Börek*, **Filo Rolls with Aubergine, Pepper and Onion** (page 36)

Gluten-free Turkish Delights

— *Mısır Ekmeği*, **Corn Bread** (page 50)
— *Adesiye*, **Pumpkin, Lentils and Chickpeas with Pomegranate Molasses** (page 143)
— *Turkish Şakşuka*, **Baked Aubergines, Courgettes, Peppers with Tomato Sauce** (page 108)
— *Kekikli, Pul Biberli Fırın Patates*, **Baked Potato Chips with Pul Biber and Oregano** (page 174)
— *Acıbadem Kurabiyesi*, **Bitter Almond Cookies** (page 238)

Plant-based Turkish Feast

— *Fellah Köftesi*, **Bulgur Kofte with Tomato and Leafy Greens Sauce** (page 106)
— *Nohut Piyazı*, **Chickpea Salad with Sumac Onions** (page 118)
— *Kırmızı Biberli Fava*, **Puréed Broad Beans with Dill and Sautéed Peppers** (page 94)
— *Imam Bayıldı*, **Stuffed Aubergines Cooked in Olive Oil** (page 154)
— *Ayva Tatlısı*, **Poached Quince Dessert (with plant-based clotted cream)** (page 228)

Turkish Comfort Food

— *Sebzeli, Mercimekli Lazanya*, **Aubergine, Lentils and Pepper Lasagne** (page 203), served with *Karışık Mevsim Salatası*, **Zingy Salad with Red Cabbage, Carrot and Sweetcorn** (page 124)
— *Fırında Patates Paçası*, **Turkish Garlicky Mashed Potatoes** (page 208), served with *Bostana Salatası*, **Orchard Salad with Pomegranate Molasses** (page 127)
— *Fırın Sütlaç*, **Baked Turkish Rice Pudding** (page 235)

Prep-ahead Turkish Feast for Entertaining

— *Zeytinyağlı Biber Dolması*, **Stuffed Peppers with Aromatic Rice** (page 144)
— *Fırında Sebzeli Karnabahar Mücveri*, **Baked Cauliflower, Peppers, Carrots, Herbs and Feta** (page 140)
— *Hellimli Sebzeli Kebap*, **Aubergine, Courgette and Halloumi Bake** (page 196)
— *Nohutlu Tepsi Mantısı*, **Baked Mantı Boats with Spiced Chickpeas** (page 204)
— *Balkabaklı, Cevizli Havuç Dilimi Baklava*, **Pumpkin and Walnut Baklava** (page 226)

Suppliers

The majority of ingredients used in Turkish cooking are widely available in most supermarkets these days; you can source a few specialty ingredients via the suppliers listed here.

UK

— **Bonvila UK:** You can find all major Turkish ingredients along with baked goods, baklava and more at this online Turkish market. *bonvila.com*

— **Odysea:** Stockists of high-quality Greek and Mediterranean products; their pomegranate molasses is one of my favourites. *odysea.com*

— **Sous Chef:** Carrying a wide range of ingredients for world cuisines, you can find many Turkish items, from pepper paste to Turkish ceramic bowls here. *souschef.co.uk*

— **Wholefood Earth:** Carry premium quality ingredients, a wide range of flour (including maize flour), wholegrains, legumes, spices, dried fruits, nuts and more. *wholefoodearth.com*

— **Ozerlat UK:** Artisanal producers of fine food, coffee and confectionery, Ozerlat UK's Turkish coffee and Turkish delight are simply the best. *ozerlat.co.uk*

US

Here are some popular Turkish online stores in the US, carrying fresh and dried goods, as well as Turkish specialty ingredients:

grandturkishbazaar.com
turkishmarketnj.com
turkishmarketonline.com
turkishfoodbasket.com

Australia

— **Gima Supermarket:** Turkish supermarket with a wide range of fresh and dried ingredients. *gimasupermarket.com.au*

— **Arzum Market:** Family-run Turkish grocery store with online delivery service, too. *arzummarket.com*

— **Grand Foods:** Suppliers of a great range of Turkish and Mediterranean products. *grandfoods.com.au*

— **Country Fresh Food Products:** Specialist food shop with range of foods from Europe, *Türkiye* (Turkey) and the Middle East. *countryfreshfoodproducts.com.au*

Index

Acknowledgements

Cookery books are a real labour of love and made with a huge, collective effort of so many amazing, talented and kind folks and I feel honoured to work with so many of them with *Sebze*. My agent Milly Reilly and JULA, thank you so much for holding my hand, believing in me and all your support for *Sebze*, it all started with you. My special thanks to you Milly, for working on the *Sebze* proposal passionately with me (even volunteering to cook the recipes along the way!) and supporting me endlessly all the way. I am very grateful our paths crossed.

Eve Marleau, thank you so much for bringing me into the Hardie Grant family, your enthusiasm for *Sebze*, and safely passing the baton to Kate Burkett. Kate, I cannot thank you enough for all your support, advice and calmness throughout the process. You kept me grounded and assured and I so enjoyed your passion for *Sebze* (as well as taking the time to cook from it – I loved seeing your *Sebze* feasts!). It was such a pleasure to work with you. My Copy Editor, Emily Preece-Morrison, my sincere thanks to you for your meticulous editing, with such care and guidance.

Sam A Harris, thank you so much for taking such beautiful, stunning photos for *Sebze* with such care, not only at our photo shoots in London, but travelling with me to *Türkiye* (Turkey) for our location shoots, too. I cherish those unforgettable memories. My family loved meeting you and were very grateful you recorded our heritage with your photos, along with beautiful food and location shoots. Esther Clark, you brought the dishes alive with such creativity and gorgeousness at our London shoots. I can't thank you enough. Tabitha Hawkins, I felt like I was at home when using your beautiful props at our shoots. Thank you so much for your vision and care. Matthew Hague, Caitlin Nuala, El Kemp, and Romy Aitken, my sincere thanks for being a part of the London shoot team. I miss our *Sebze* feasts and feel very lucky to work with you all.

Nic & Lou, thank you so very much for bringing *Sebze* to life with your gorgeous design and eye for detail. Also my special thanks for your stunning illustrations in the *Sebze* chapter openers.

My dear parents, Orhan and Gülçin, who both passed away recently. You have been my biggest inspiration. Thank you mum and dad for your unconditional love, and for infusing us with a love of Turkish food. I am very grateful for this special connection with you, appreciation of food and caring for one another through food. Mum knew I was writing *Sebze* and was so excited for our bountiful vegetarian dishes to take centre stage, even during her fragile health. She had seen all my tested recipes during our video calls and would always show her support, wearing her beautiful smile and words of encouragement. I hope you are proud of *Sebze*. *Anneciğim, babacığım* – you are always in my heart.

My dearest sister Öznur and Mehmet, Defne and sevgili Nihal Abla (and Zen Ceramics, for the beautiful plates you let us use in Istanbul), for all your love and amazing support while shooting. Many thanks sevgili Cengiz dayı, Naciye abla and Neriman teyze for joining us in Istanbul, too. It was a very special shoot with you all. Dearest Şefika Teyze, Abdullah Enişte, Suphi Abi, Mebrure Abla and sevgili Aynur, for coming over to Antakya to join us at Meriç Çiftliği. Having you with us meant the world to me - *çok teşekkür ederim*.

A very special thanks to my dear friend Hadice Nalçabasmaz and Meriç Çiftliği, in Altınözü, Antakya, for hosting us, the photo shoot, and for your incredible hospitality. Being at the bountiful, beautiful Meriç Çiftliği with family very much reminded me of being at my grandmother's home in Antakya, and created unforgettable memories for us all. It was very special and poignant to return to Antakya as we prepared *mezes* together around the table like we used to. I was right at home and felt gratitude and hope for the future. It will be a long journey to recovery after the earthquake, but with the passionate, dedicated Antakyalı like dear Hadice, I am hopeful that in time we will get our beloved hometown back - *çok teşekkür ederim*.

My dearest friend Susie Bossard, there are really not enough words how much your friendship means to me – with almost every tested recipe, I appeared by your door and you always gave honest feedback with Keith. Thank you for always being there and offering your love and support.

Sevgili Gülsüm Genç Koç, for working tirelessly on the corn bread recipe with me and for all your insights, *çok teşekkür ederim Gülsüm'cüğüm*. Dear Rosemary Gill, Bee Harrison, Gillian Burns, Nejla Engin, Heleen Koolhof and Jonelle Salter, for very kindly testing the recipes and your dear friendship. Ilgen'ciğim (and to Cotton & Olive, for the beautiful Turkish fabrics) and Handan'cığım, for our endless chats, your lovely ideas, friendship and inspiration. Dear Judith and Gavin, Hande, Ece, Jenny, Öniz, Sam, Ellie, Rodica, Lisa, Mark and Jolee, for all of your support and friendship. It means a lot.

Dear Diana Henry, many thanks for your kind words and support for *Sebze*, it has meant so much to me. Thank you dear Irina Georgescu, for our early chats on this project and all your kindness and support. Dear Caroline Eden, Ruby Tandoh, Meliz Berg, Melek Erdal, Georgina Hayden, Sabrina Ghayour, Joe Woodhouse, Amy Shepphard, Saliha Mahmood Ahmed, Ghillie Başan, Joudie Kalla, Mallika Basu, Jenny Linford, Lucy Battersby, Rosemary Gill, Karen Cassady and Elena & Melisa Koyunseven, thank you for your kind words of support at the proposal stage and beyond for *Sebze*. Dear Sahrap Soysal, for championing regional Turkish cuisine and your valuable insights. You are an inspiration. Leanne Kitchen, for all your kindness and help.

Last but not least, my dearest husband, Angus'cuğum; thank you for being my rock and for all your love, patience and support. Canlarımız Mark Can and Emma Gülçin, thank you for bearing with me during endless recipe testing. It makes me so happy to see your interest in food. I couldn't have written this book without you – *çok teşekkür ederim*, I love you lots.

About the Author

About the Author

Özlem Warren is a Turkish food writer and cookery teacher. She frequently travels to teach Turkish cookery in the USA, *Türkiye* (Turkey), UK and Jordan. Her debut cookbook, *Özlem's Turkish Table, Recipes from My Homeland*, was published in 2019 and won the 2020 Gourmand Best in the World Award in Food Heritage. Her recipes and articles are published in major newspapers and magazines including the *Waitrose Food Magazine*, *Waitrose Weekend*, *The New York Times Cooking*, *Milk Street Magazine*, *Hurriyet Daily News* and *Sabah Daily*. She hosts culinary and cultural tours to *Türkiye* (Turkey) and participates in prestigious events such as the Taste of London, The London Book Fair, the International Edinburgh Book Festival and various food festivals to promote Turkish cuisine and culture.

Özlem shares her recipes, events and travels on her Instagram page: @ozlems_turkish_table

Published in 2024 by Hardie Grant Books,
an imprint of Hardie Grant Publishing

Hardie Grant Books (London)
5th & 6th Floors
52–54 Southwark Street
London SE1 1UN

Hardie Grant Books (Melbourne)
Building 1, 658 Church Street
Richmond, Victoria 3121

hardiegrantbooks.com

British Library Cataloguing-in-Publication
Data. A catalogue record for this book
is available from the British Library.

Sebze
ISBN: 9781784886486

10 9 8 7 6 5 4 3 2 1

Publishing Director: Kajal Mistry
Commissioning Editor: Eve Marleau
Project Editor: Kate Burkett
Design: Emma Wells, Studio Nic&Lou
Photography: Sam A Harris
Photographer's assistant: Matthew Hague
Food stylist: Esther Clark
Food stylist's assistants: Caitlin Nuala, El Kemp and Romy Aitken
Prop stylist: Tabitha Hawkins
Copy Editor: Emily Preece-Morrison
Proofreader: Emily Rogers
Indexer: Cathy Heath
Production Controller: Sabeena Atchia

Colour Reproduction by p2d
Printed and bound in China by Leo Paper Products Ltd.